D1434147

THE FROGS
AND OTHER GREEK PLAYS

The Heritage of Literature Series

This series incorporates titles under the following headings: Travel and Adventure, Animal Stories, Fiction, Modern Classics, Short Stories, Prose Writing, Drama, Myths and Legends, Poetry.

Other titles in the Drama Section of the series include:

FOUR GREEK PLAYS *Kenneth McLeish*
THE KNIGHT OF THE BURNING PESTLE *Beaumont and Fletcher*
THE LADY WITH A LAMP *Reginald Berkeley*
RICHARD OF BORDEAUX *Gordon Daviot*
SHE STOOPS TO CONQUER *Oliver Goldsmith*
ADVENTURE STORY *Terence Rattigan*
THE WINSLOW BOY *Terence Rattigan*
THE ROYAL HUNT OF THE SUN *Peter Shaffer*
THE SCHOOL FOR SCANDAL and THE CRITIC *R. B. Sheridan*
THE LONG SUNSET *R. C. Sherriff*
TRAITORS' GATE *Morna Stuart*
OUR TOWN *Thornton Wilder*
THE SKIN OF OUR TEETH *Thornton Wilder*

A complete list of the series is available on request.

The Frogs
and other Greek Plays

Aristophanes:
THE BIRDS
THE FROGS

Aeschylus:
PROMETHEUS BOUND

Euripides:
MEDEA

translated and adapted by
KENNETH McLEISH

Drawings by
TERENCE GREER

LONGMAN

LONGMAN GROUP LIMITED
London

Associated companies, branches and representatives throughout the world

© Kenneth McLeish 1970

First published 1970
SBN 582 34514 6

PRINTED IN GREAT BRITAIN BY
RICHARD CLAY (THE CHAUCER PRESS), LTD.
BUNGAY, SUFFOLK

CONTENTS

TRANSLATOR'S NOTE

This book, like its predecessor *Four Greek Plays*,[1] contains adaptations of two Greek tragedies framed by comedies of Aristophanes. This volume has been built round Aristophanes' *Frogs*, perhaps the best loved of all his plays, and the tragedies—Euripides' *Medea* and Aeschylus' *Prometheus Bound*—provide a relevant background for Aristophanes' comments and criticisms in the second half of his play.

At an early stage I decided it was pointless to translate Aeschylus into prose: the rhythm and compression of verse seemed essential if the task was to be attempted at all. This meant, in all fairness, that Euripides had to be treated the same way; I have, however, tried to make my own verse mirror the differing style of each author. *The Birds* and *The Frogs* have been translated into prose, with the choral sections in "light verse", suitable for musical setting.

Some sections of *The Birds* and *The Frogs* have been cut or paraphrased, and *Medea* has been reduced where the mythology threatened to overload the text. But I have left *Prometheus Bound* more or less intact, believing that a great part of its effect lies in Aeschylus' use of unusual words and evocative place-names. Complete versions of the plays are available in many modern translations, notably those in the Penguin Classics series.

---

[1] The introduction to that volume covers the essential details of Greek theatre and the historical background of the plays. Fuller accounts are available in Pickard-Cambridge's *The Theatre of Dionysus* and *Dramatic Festivals in Athens*, and readers are also referred to the relevant chapter in Bamber Gascoigne's *World Theatre*, which has some outstanding illustrations.

THE BIRDS

NOTE

This play was first produced in Athens in 414 B.C., six years after *Peace*. Both plays were written in the shadow of the Peloponnesian War, but they have absolutely nothing else in common. *Peace* is a savage satire on the generals and politicians who kept the war going for their own ends; *The Birds* is a fairy tale, whose escapist theme and gentle humour must have been a welcome relaxation for war-weary Athenians.

The Birds is one of Aristophanes' longest and most lyrical plays. Its choruses are among the finest he ever wrote, and the play is notable for the large number of knockabout characters who appear in the second half. Despite the absence of satire, Aristophanes' invention is as exuberant as ever: who would think, for example, that his Prometheus (p. 50) is the same character as Aeschylus' tragic hero? And who but Aristophanes could have dreamed up the idea of starving out the gods by stealing their sacrifices? In much of its comic detail the play is on a level with his greatest work.

The actual construction of the play is very loose and fluid. It is like a modern pantomime, where the plot is a peg on which all kinds of extravagant interludes can be hung. Like a pantomime, too, it depends for its effect on colourful costumes and lavish stage display; and like a pantomime it contains lyricism and burlesque, high poetry and slapstick farce, in almost equal proportions.

The Birds was written in one of the worst periods of the war, and many members of the audience must have felt real sympathy for Pisthetairos and Euelpides, who decided to leave Athens for ever, and find a new home somewhere known only to the birds. . . .

THE BIRDS

Characters in order of appearance:

EUELPIDES ⎫
PISTHETAIROS ⎭ *elderly Athenian citizens*
Tereus' SLAVE, *a running-bird*
TEREUS, *a hoopoe, king of the birds*
PROKNE (*later Chairis*), *a flute-playing nightingale*
PRIEST
POET
PROPHET
METON, *a mathematician*
AMBASSADOR
BARRISTER
MESSENGER
WATCHMAN
HERALD
IRIS, *a goddess*
WARLIKE BOY
KINESIAS, *a lyric poet with a lisp*
INFORMER
PROMETHEUS
POSEIDON
HERAKLES
TRIBALLOS, *a foreign god*
QUEENIE, *a beautiful maiden*
CHORUS OF BIRDS

Note: When the CHORUS speak as a chorus, they are
called simply CHORUS. But there are also single voices,
parts taken by individual birds: these are marked
CHORUS A, CHORUS B and CHORUS C.

THE BIRDS

SCENE ONE

The foot of a barren cliff in the desert. PISTHE-
TAIROS *and* EUELPIDES *come in, each with a bird
on his shoulder. They look footsore and weary.*

EUELPIDES *to his bird*: What was that? On, did you
say? To that tree?

PISTHETAIROS: This one's cawing "back". (*caws*) Back,
back!

EUELPIDES: Look, we're just wasting our time walking
up and down like this. We're lost.

PISTHETAIROS: Fancy coming all this way, at the whim
of a bloody raven!

EUELPIDES: And what about me? Worn my toes to the
bone, just to please a motheaten old crow!

PISTHETAIROS: Have you any idea where we are?

EUELPIDES: *You* said our country would be round here
somewhere . . . the one we've come all this way to find.
Well, where is it?

PISTHETAIROS *bitterly*: How should I know?

EUELPIDES: Oh hell!

PISTHETAIROS: Go to hell if you like—it'd certainly be
quicker.

EUELPIDES: I'd like to see Philokrates in hell . . . that
bird-seller in the market. He told us he'd give us guides
to take us to Tereus, the king of the birds who changed
from a man into a hoopoe. All he really wanted was to
pass his feathered friends on to us. Feathered friends?
Feathered fiends, more like! All they can do is bite. (*To
his bird*) Now what are you pointing at? That cliff?

6

We're certainly not going that way—can't you see it says "no road"?

PISTHETAIROS: It's hopeless.

EUELPIDES: Well, what's your raven got to say now?

PISTHETAIROS: Just a minute . . .

He listens.

Oh no! She says she's going to peck my finger off!

EUELPIDES: I told you it'd be easier to go to the dogs. There's no sign of birds anywhere.

He suddenly sees the audience, and steps forward to speak to them.

Er . . . ladies and gentlemen, I suppose you're wondering what on earth this is all about? Well, you see, my friend and I are trying to get away from Athens. All these foreigners bursting a bloodvessel to get in, all we want to do is get out! Don't misunderstand me, though: we've nothing against Athens. It's a great place . . . freedom, wealth, happiness, justice for everyone. That's the trouble: justice! Grasshoppers sing for a couple of months, and that's that. But Athenians sit on jury-service for a year at a time, chirping and twittering on tiny points of law. Stupid, we thought it was. So we picked up our household gods, and set out to find a place without a law-courts, where we could retire to a quiet life. Tereus . . . he's the man we're looking for. Or bird, rather. He flies about everywhere: he'll have seen the place we want.

PISTHETAIROS *suddenly*: Hey!

EUELPIDES: What?

PISTHETAIROS: My raven's off again . . . pointing up, now.

EUELPIDES: Yes . . . and so's my crow. (To *his bird*) What is it, then? What are you trying to tell me?

7

He listens, then turns to PISTHETAIROS *in great excitement.*

We've arrived, that's what it is! The birds are around here somewhere. If we make a noise, they'll come out.

PISTHETAIROS: All right . . . give the rock a kick.

EUELPIDES: Who me? You knock it with your head . . . that'll make twice the noise!

PISTHETAIROS: Oh, hit it with a stone, then.

EUELPIDES *does so.*

EUELPIDES: Hullo! Hullo! Anyone at home?

PISTHETAIROS: What d'you mean, hullo? It's a hoopoe you're calling . . . yoohoo, you should be shouting.

EUELPIDES: Oh, all right. (*exaggeratedly*) Yoohoo! Hoo-poooe! Yoooo-hoooo!

A door opens in the cliff, and Tereus' SLAVE *comes out.*

SLAVE: Yes? Who wants my master?

EUELPIDES: My god, what a beak!

SLAVE: Oh no! Bird-catchers again! Not today, thank you!

EUELPIDES: Oh, very funny. How d'you even know we're *men*?

SLAVE: What are you then?

EUELPIDES: Birds, both of us. I'm a . . . a Dung-dropping Collywobbler.

SLAVE: And what about your friend?

PISTHETAIROS: I'm a Rarely Spotted Twit.

EUELPIDES: And what about *you* . . . if you don't mind me asking?

SLAVE *with dignity*: I'm a butler bird.

EUELPIDES: How d'you mean, a butler bird?

SLAVE: When my master changed into a hoopoe, he

8

begged me to change as well, so that I could go on serving
him.

EUELPIDES: So birds need servants now?

SLAVE: Oh yes, you'd be surprised. He quite often has a
craving for some of his old mortal food. "Sardines!" he'll
cry, for example, "Bring me some sardines!" So I run
and fetch him some. Or "Beans!" he'll say, and I get him
some beans. It's run, run, run, all day long.

EUELPIDES: He gets a good run for his money, then,
does he?

There is an embarrassed silence all round.

Well, just run inside, will you, and ask your master to
come out.

SLAVE: I can't. He's just had his dinner . . . two worms
and a barley-corn . . . and he'll be taking a nap.

EUELPIDES: Wake him up, then.

SLAVE: I know he won't like it. Still, if you insist . . .

He goes inside and shuts the door.

PISTHETAIROS: Phew! That was a near thing! Why
don't you watch what you're saying?

EUELPIDES: He's scared away my raven.

PISTHETAIROS: You let it go, you mean. Coward!

EUELPIDES: All right, where's yours?

PISTHETAIROS: Er . . .

EUELPIDES: Well?

PISTHETAIROS: It . . . er . . . flew away.

EUELPIDES: Flew away, did it? Now who's a coward?

TEREUS *from inside, grandly*: "Ope me the door. Your
king is faring forth."

*There is a fanfare, the door is thrown open, and he
comes out.*

9

EUELPIDES: Good lord, what a creature! Look at his plumes . . . and his crest!

TEREUS: Someone was asking for me?

EUELPIDES: It's all right . . . poor old thing . . .

TEREUS: Are you mocking me because my feathers are a little threadbare? I'll have you know . . . "I once was mortal too." (Aeschylus).

EUELPIDES: Oh, we're not laughing at you.

TEREUS: What then?

EUELPIDES: Your beak.

TEREUS: Ah! You find my beak odd. Well, it's all Sophocles' fault. If he hadn't said I turned into a bird . . . in that tragedy . . . the *Tereus* . .

EUELPIDES: You're not Tereus, are you? Are you a bird, or not?

TEREUS: I'm a bird all right.

EUELPIDES: Where are your feathers, then?

TEREUS: Moulted.

EUELPIDES: Moulted? Aren't you well?

TEREUS: No, no. We all moult at this time of year . . . we grow new feathers later on. All right, I'm a bird . . . what are you?

EUELPIDES: Us? Mortals.

TEREUS: Where from?

EUELPIDES: Athens . . . you know, "Where the big ships come from".

TEREUS: Athens, eh? You're jurymen, then?

EUELPIDES: Good heavens, no! Anti-jurymen, that's us.

TEREUS: But why have you come *here*?

PISTHETAIROS: We came to see you.

TEREUS: Me? Why?

PISTHETAIROS: You used to be a man . . .

EUELPIDES: Just like us.

PISTHETAIROS: You used to owe money . . .

EUELPIDES: Just like us.

PISTHETAIROS: And you didn't like paying up . . .

EUELPIDES: Just like us.

PISTHETAIROS: Then you changed into a bird . . . and since then you've flown everywhere, seen everything, found out everything. So we've come to ask you if you know a comfortable, woolly country we can wrap ourselves up in, and live in peace.

TEREUS: Somewhere greater than Athens?

EUELPIDES: Not greater, just more suitable . . . the sort of place where your greatest worry is a neighbour coming round and saying: "Don't forget you and your family are invited to the wedding tomorrow. Come early, don't forget . . . and if you fail me now, don't ever come crawling round when I'm in trouble!" That sort of place.

TEREUS: H'm . . . There is one place, down by the Red Sea . . .

EUELPIDES: Egypt? You must be mad! Is there nowhere in Greece?

TEREUS: What about Lepreon?

EUELPIDES: Lepreon? No thanks . . . I can't stand tropical diseases.

TEREUS: Opuntioi in Locris?

EUELPIDES *in an exaggerated Scots accent*: A punt ahoy in Loch Ness? Och, mon, you're crazy!

TEREUS: I can't think of anywhere else . . .

EUELPIDES *suddenly*: What's it like here?

TEREUS: Here?

EUELPIDES: Yes. What sort of life d'you lead here, you birds?

11

TEREUS: Oh, not bad, really. We don't use money, for a start.

EUELPIDES: That's a good idea . . . if you've got as little as I have.

TEREUS: We flit about from twig to twig, nibbling poppy-seeds, banqueting on barley, and roystering on rice-cakes.

EUELPIDES: H'm. Sounds too much like a wedding-feast for me.

PISTHETAIROS *suddenly*: I've got it, I've got it! This really is a good idea! Listen to me . . . you'll never regret it!

TEREUS *startled*: Eh? What d'you mean?

PISTHETAIROS: I'll tell you what to do. (*pointedly*) First of all, stop flying around with your beak wide open . . .

TEREUS *shutting his beak quickly*: All right, there. What next?

PISTHETAIROS: Build one single city.

TEREUS: A city? What would birds want with a city?

PISTHETAIROS: What would they want . . . ? Look down here a minute.

He points to the ground. TEREUS *stares at it fixedly.*

TEREUS: Yes.

PISTHETAIROS *pointing at the sky*: Now up here.

TEREUS: Yes.

PISTHETAIROS: Now turn your head round . . . right round . . .

TEREUS: There . . . ow!

PISTHETAIROS: What can you see?

TEREUS *mystified*: Nothing. Clouds . . . sky . . .

PISTHETAIROS: There, then! That's where you want

to build, right in the middle of the sky.

TEREUS: Whatever for?

PISTHETAIROS: Don't you see? It's halfway between earth and heaven. You could hold the gods to ransom.

TEREUS: I don't quite follow . . .

PISTHETAIROS: Look: when we go from Athens to Sparta, we cross the Isthmus and pass through the Corinthian Canal. The Corinthians charge us duty, and make a fat profit. Well, when men sacrifice to the gods down *there*, it has to pass through *here* to get up *there*. Now d'you see? Unless the gods pay you taxes, you stop their sacrifices and starve them out!

TEREUS: It's brilliant . . . quite magnificent! A genius, that's what you are! We'll do it . . . that is, providing the other birds agree.

PISTHETAIROS: Who'll ask them?

TEREUS: You will.

PISTHETAIROS: But I don't speak . . .

TEREUS: It's all right, I've taught them Greek. Just a minute while I call them.

PISTHETAIROS: How?

TEREUS: No problem. I step into the thicket here, and wake up my nightingale. As soon as they hear her singing, they'll come running.

PISTHETAIROS: Hurry up, then. Wake her up, quickly.

TEREUS *steps forward and invokes the nightingale.*

TEREUS:
Come, my dear one; waken now
And fill the woods with your honey-song.
Sing, my love, to delight us.
Sing till you charm the gods themselves;

13

Sing till the golden sky resounds;
Apollo will answer your silver song,
Plucking sweet harmonies to echo you.
Sing, my love, to delight us.

After a short pause a flute begins to play, softly and irresistibly.

EUELPIDES: Hey!
PISTHETAIROS: Shh'
EUELPIDES: Why?
PISTHETAIROS: He hasn't finished.
TEREUS:
Come, all of you: come and hear me now.
Birds of the meadowlands,
Birds of the wind-swept lakes;
Garden-birds, feasting on berries
Or swooping to secret nests; water-birds,
Waders and dippers, who love the soft green plains;
Sea-birds—gulls and terns
And harsh-voiced cormorants—
Leave your pastures, and come and hear me now.
A stranger is here, an old, wise stranger,
With a young man's scheme to benefit us all.
Come, all of you, and hear what he has to say.

The flute continues to play. Gradually, from a distance, but coming always nearer, there is the sound of an approaching flock of birds.

PISTHETAIROS: Can you see any birds?
EUELPIDES: Nothing! I've stared at the sky till my eyes are popping, but I can't see anything. It looks as though Tereus was wasting his time.

A bird appears suddenly behind him, making him jump.

14

CHORUS C: Tweet!

EUELPIDES *admiringly*: Hey! What a magnificent creature! What's it called?

PISTHETAIROS: Ask Tereus.

TEREUS: It's an uncommon bird . . . lives in the marshes.

EUELPIDES: It's superb . . . what a magnificent red!

TEREUS: That's right; it's a redshank.

More and more birds begin to come in. EUELPIDES *gets very excited.*

EUELPIDES: Hey, look!

PISTHETAIROS: What now?

EUELPIDES: I've never seen one of those before.

PISTHETAIROS: What on earth is it?

TEREUS: An Arabian stork.

PISTHETAIROS: I thought it reminded me of a camel.

EUELPIDES: Look, look, here's another!

PISTHETAIROS: Good lord! What *is* it?

TEREUS: A Great Hairy Twit.

EUELPIDES: What a cloud of birds! I can hardly see the stage.

TEREUS: There's a partridge . . . and there's a swallow . . . a mallard . . . a great crested grebe . . .

PISTHETAIROS: What's that one?

TEREUS: A kingfisher.

EUELPIDES: And what are all those?

TEREUS *rapidly*: Cockatoo, turtle-dove, plover, screech-owl, meadow-lark, wood-pigeon, falcon, sparrow-hawk, cuckoo, flamingo, redshank, robin, kestrel, dipper, bee-eater, vulture, woodpecker . . .

PISTHETAIROS: Stop, stop! I can't take in any more. Look at them all chirping and fluttering round . . .

EUELPIDES: I hope they're friendly.

PISTHETAIROS: Hey! I don't think they are!

The CHORUS *begin to bunch together. They look distinctly menacing.*

CHORUS A: Hoo-hoo-who was it who called us here? Where is he?

TEREUS: Here. It was me.

CHORUS B: Why? What d'you want to tell us?

TEREUS: A marvellous, brilliant, exciting scheme! Two clever planners have come to help us . . .

CHORUS: Who? What? Where? How?

TEREUS: Two ambassadors from men, with the idea for a mighty scheme . . .

CHORUS C: You scoundrel! What d'you mean?

TEREUS: There's no need to be alarmed.

CHORUS A: What have you done to us?

TEREUS: I've taken in a couple of strangers . . .

CHORUS A: Taken them in?

TEREUS: Yes.

CHORUS B: You mean they're here, now . . . (*shuddering*) *among* us?

TEREUS: Yes.

CHORUS:
    Oh, oh, oh!

CHORUS A:
    We've been betrayed; we've been deceived;
    Of our leader's trust we've been bereaved—
    Without just cause he's defied our laws;
    It's the cruellest blow that we've ever received!

CHORUS:
    Oh, oh, oh!

CHORUS B:
    We're caught in his trap; we're snared in his nets;

16

He's betrayed us all, without any regrets—
Two men are here, men whom we fear,
For they kill us and eat us, and make us their pets!

CHORUS:
Oh, oh, oh!

CHORUS A: We'll deal with him later. First we'd better get rid of *them*. Kill them! Tear them to pieces!

PISTHETAIROS: Oh dear! It looks as though we're done for.

EUELPIDES: It's all your fault. Why did I let you talk me into it?

PISTHETAIROS: You wanted to come.

EUELPIDES: To come, yes—but not to come to grief! We'll be crying for mercy soon, I'm telling you.

PISTHETAIROS: Oh no we won't.

EUELPIDES: What?

PISTHETAIROS: How can we cry when our eyes have been pecked out?

EUELPIDES: Oh, thank you very much . . . that's a great help!

CHORUS:
Close in, close in, close in for the kill;
Sharpen your claws, and beak and bill;
Fluff out your feathers; come on, surround
Them, tear them, trample them into the ground!

No mountain peak, no crashing wave,
No soaring cloud their lives will save.
Prepare yourselves—more courage still—
Get ready now, then kill, kill, kill!

CHORUS B: What are we waiting for?

CHORUS A: Where's the wing commander?

EUELPIDES *going*: Oh well, that's that. No point hanging around . . .

PISTHETAIROS: Where are you going? Stay here!

EUELPIDES: Stay here, and be torn to bits?

PISTHETAIROS: You don't think they'll let you get away, do you?

EUELPIDES: Well, what else can we do?

PISTHETAIROS: Stay and fight, of course. Here, take this dustbin lid.

EUELPIDES: What for?

PISTHETAIROS: A shield, you idiot! And here's a skewer . . . use it to scare them off . . . or spit them with it, if they come too close.

EUELPIDES: What about my eyes?

PISTHETAIROS: Here: wear this sieve for a helmet . . .

He starts fastening the various pieces of "armour" on to EUELPIDES.

EUELPIDES *sarcastically*: Proper little Nikias, aren't you?

PISTHETAIROS: Look out! Here they come!

CHORUS:
Forward, forward, beaks at the ready;
Stab them, bite them, tear them! Steady!

They rush forward, but TEREUS *places himself in the way.*

TEREUS: Stop, stop! What's the matter with you? They haven't done anything. Leave them alone!

CHORUS C: Why should we?

TEREUS: They've come to help us.

CHORUS B: Help us? You must be joking! Birds and men have always been enemies.

TEREUS: Maybe. But a wise man learns even from his enemies.

CHORUS B: Eh?

TEREUS: It's not your friends that teach you to be careful who you trust . . . it's your enemies. It's their enemies that teach cities to build high walls and vast great fleets, not their friends—and isn't it walls and fleets that protect their wives, their children, and all they own?

CHORUS A *reluctantly*: All right, there's no harm in listening to them. But it had better be worth hearing, that's all.

PISTHETAIROS *aside to* EUELPIDES: They're drawing back. Give ground a little.

TEREUS: You'll see I was right. Have I ever let you down before?

CHORUS C: I suppose not.

CHORUS B: All right then.

PISTHETAIROS: O.K. It's all over. Put down your shield, and sheathe your skewer.

EUELPIDES: Phew! I really thought we'd had it that time.

CHORUS A: Back to your ranks! Sheathe your anger; put away your fury. We're going to listen to them. Tereus . . .

TEREUS: Yes?

CHORUS A: Who are they, and where are they from?

TEREUS: They're from Greece, and they've brought us some real Greek wisdom.

CHORUS B: But why us? Why visit the birds?

TEREUS: They want to live here, and share our life.

CHORUS B: Whatever for?

TEREUS: Just wait and see. You'll like their ideas.

CHORUS C: They'll have to be good, to have brought them all this way. What *do* they want . . . help for their friends, or support against their enemies?

TEREUS: Neither. They want to bring us wealth and happiness, and make us kings of earth and sky and heaven.

CHORUS A: You're joking!

TEREUS: No, no. You wait and see. They're wise, and sane, full of clever ideas, wily, sly . . .

CHORUS B: All right, all right. We'll judge that for ourselves.

TEREUS: Here, slave! Take these gentlemen's weapons and hang them up in the kitchen. (*To* PISTHETAIROS) Now, my friend, tell them what you've just told me.

PISTHETAIROS: No, not one word.

TEREUS: *What?*

PISTHETAIROS: They'll have to make a peace-treaty first. No biting, no kicking, no gouging . . .

CHORUS C: All right, all right. Get on with it!

PISTHETAIROS: Cross your heart.

CHORUS C: Oh . . . cross my heart.

PISTHETAIROS: Dismiss the troops.

The LEADER *of the Chorus signs to the* HERALD, *who blows a fanfare.*

HERALD: Hear this, hear this! All fighting birds to return their weapons to the stores, go back to barracks, and wait for further orders.

Some of the CHORUS *leave, while the rest prepare to listen.*

CHORUS:
Man has always been a most deceitful creature;
This has always been his most consistent feature.

None the less, speak out,
And tell us what you advise us.
Say what it's all about,
And with your wit surprise us.

CHORUS C: Come on, sir. We promise to listen . . .

PISTHETAIROS: I'm bursting to start; I've got a speech boiling up inside, and any moment now . . . Slave, fetch me an ivy-wreath, and some water to wash my hands.

EUELPIDES: Ah! Going to have dinner, are we?

PISTHETAIROS: Dinner, no. A feast of words, fat and sumptuous. . . . Hrrm! Hrrm! My friends, I grieve for you. Once you were kings . . .

CHORUS A: Kings? Us? Who of?

PISTHETAIROS: Me, him, Zeus himself. You were here before all the gods, before all the heroes and giants, even before the earth itself.

CHORUS B: The earth? How d'you work that out?

PISTHETAIROS: Haven't you ever thought about it? Don't you know any history—haven't you even read Aesop? You must remember his fable about the lark, who was born before the earth existed. When his father died, he was at his wits' end because there was nowhere to dig a grave. In the end all he could do was *imagine* one, and bury his father inside his own head.

EUELPIDES: And that's why graves have a *headstone* nowadays!

PISTHETAIROS: And obviously, if you were here before the gods, you're older than they are, and you ought to rule them, instead of them you.

EUELPIDES: You'd better sharpen up your beaks, too. Zeus won't give you his throne without a fight, I'm warning you.

PISTHETAIROS: Besides, it wasn't the gods who ruled

21

men in the olden days, it was you.

CHORUS A: But how?

PISTHETAIROS: In all sorts of ways. The cock used to be the Great King of all men. And even now, when he crows, everyone jumps up at once . . . blacksmiths, tanners, armourers, cobblers, bakers, woodcarvers, everyone!

EUELPIDES *starts reminiscing. Everyone listens with growing impatience.*

EUELPIDES: You're telling me! I blame it all on the cock. I used to have a beautiful cloak, but thanks to him . . . I'd been to a christening, you see, and just happened to have had a drink or two. I was dozing off when a cock crew, just before dinner. Naturally I thought it was dawn, and set off home. But as soon as I stuck my nose out of the gate . . . bam! Knocked on the head by a robber, stripped of my lovely new cloak . . . and all because of a cock who hadn't learned to tell the time!

PISTHETAIROS: After the cock it was a buzzard who ruled the Greeks.

CHORUS A: A buzzard . . . ruled the *Greeks?*

PISTHETAIROS: Yes—and even now, when a buzzard swoops down on them, people bow.

EUELPIDES *as before*: That's true. I remember once . . . I'd lost my purse, and the only safe place to keep my small change was in my mouth. I was walking home, quiet as you like, when suddenly a huge great buzzard swoops down at me. Of course I bow down and duck—and swallow the lot!

PISTHETAIROS: Men still need the cuckoo to tell them when it's spring. You don't catch any fenland farmer sowing till the first cuckoo's appeared.

22

EUELPIDES: Yes: but then fenlanders were always a bit cuckoo, if you ask me!

PISTHETAIROS: You've all seen statues of Zeus . . . you know, Zeus the *new* king of the gods. Well, even he has an eagle perched on his sceptre, to keep an eye on him. And Apollo has a hawk, and Athene an owl.

EUELPIDES: So they do! D'you know, I've always wondered why.

PISTHETAIROS *annoyed*: Do you mind?

EUELPIDES: I'm sorry. Do go on.

PISTHETAIROS: Another thing: men never really swear by the gods. When they say "By Zeus" they really mean "By Goose"—and you must have heard people exclaim, "Well, stone the crows!" All this proves that you were once kings, not what you are now: hunted, pursued and mocked, trapped, netted, plucked, stuck on a lime-board and sold. They're not satisfied with spitting and roasting you, either—they sprinkle grated cheese and herbs all over you, and serve you up soaked in scalding gravy, as though you'd no rights at all!

CHORUS:
 This has been a most distressing story.
 To think we've lost our fathers' ancient glory!
 None the less, kind fate
 Has sent you here to lead us;
 You, sir, can make us great—
 So help us, guide us, feed us!

CHORUS B: How can we set about getting all this back? I can't wait to be a king again!

PISTHETAIROS: First, build *one* city for all the birds, well fortified. Then put up a strong brick wall, right across the middle of the sky.

TEREUS: I can hardly wait!

23

PISTHETAIROS: When it's finished, we'll demand that Zeus abdicates. If he won't, we'll have a crusade to win back our rights, and close the wall. No god to pass through from heaven to earth; no more visiting the ladies down below—no more godultery. Hit them where it hurts most! Then we'll send a messenger bird down to men, and tell them to sacrifice to us now, not the gods.

CHORUS A: Yes, that's all very well . . . but how will they recognise us as gods, if all we do is fly about like we did before?

PISTHETAIROS: Zeus and Hermes fly about, don't they —and you're not telling me *they're* not recognised as gods?

EUELPIDES: All right, so the gods fly about. But so do Zeus's thunderbolts. Suppose he throws one down at men, and frightens them back into submission?

PISTHETAIROS: If they need to be frightened before they'll worship anyone, we'll send an army of seed-gatherers to strip their corn-fields. *Then* let them ask the gods for a free delivery! And we'll send crows to peck out the eyes of their sheep and cattle—*then* let them beg the gods to cure them!

EUELPIDES: Hey! Let me sell *my* oxen first!

PISTHETAIROS: On the other hand, if they make us their gods, we'll grant them all sorts of blessings.

TEREUS: Such as?

PISTHETAIROS: Locusts: they won't need to be afraid of them any more. One squadron of owls, and that's the end of them. No more midges or gnats sucking away the fruit-crop; we'll have a battalion of thrushes on pest control.

TEREUS: But how can we give them wealth? That's all they really care about.

24

PISTHETAIROS: That's easy. We can fly about overhead and survey new goldmines for them. We can
inspect all their trade-routes in advance, and they won't
ever lose a ship.

TEREUS: Why not?

PISTHETAIROS: Weather forecasting. We'll tell 'em:
"It's stormy ahead; don't sail today", or "It's set fair;
now's the time for your voyage."

TEREUS: What about good health? That comes from
the gods; we can't give them that.

PISTHETAIROS: That won't matter. So long as they're
making money they won't worry about their health. Only
poor men have time to be ill.

TEREUS: It's marvellous! We'll be far better kings than
Zeus.

PISTHETAIROS: Yes, far better. In the first place, they
won't need to build stone temples with golden gates any
more . . . their bird-gods will be quite happy with a
thicket or a thorn-bush. There'll be no need to go to Delphi
or Ammon to sacrifice . . . they can give us their offer-
ings wherever they are, just by throwing a handful of
barley into the nearest clump of bushes, and praying for
whatever they want.

CHORUS:
Excited by this mighty plan,
We give our solemn vow:
If we are led by this wise old man,
The gods who rule us now
Will soon, because of his counsels wise and bold,
Give us back the crown they so unjustly hold.

PISTHETAIROS: All right, don't let's waste any more
time talking—it's time for action.

TEREUS: My friends, just step inside my nest a moment,

will you? It's only a few twigs and branches, but it's home to me. Just a minute, though: you haven't told us your names yet.

PISTHETAIROS: Pisthetairos.

EUELPIDES: Euelpides, from Krios.

TEREUS: You're both welcome.

PISTHETAIROS: Thank you.

TEREUS: Step this way, would you?

EUELPIDES: *After* you . . .

PISTHETAIROS: Just a moment! How can we live here with you, when we haven't any wings?

TEREUS: That's no problem. We've plenty inside.

PISTHETAIROS: All right. Slaves, pick up the luggage, and follow me.

CHORUS A: Tereus!

TEREUS: Now what?

CHORUS A: Take these gentlemen inside by all means, and give them some wings. But send us out our nightingale, our sweetest nightingale, to sing with us.

PISTHETAIROS: Yes, good idea. Call her out here.

EUELPIDES: Yes, do! We're all dying to see her.

TEREUS: All right, if you say so.

He opens the door, and calls:

Prokne, my love, come out and say hello to our visitors.

The NIGHTINGALE *comes out.*

PISTHETAIROS: Zeus, what a beautiful bird! How soft her feathers are!

EUELPIDES: I'd like to ruffle 'em up a bit!

PISTHETAIROS: What a lovely head!

EUELPIDES: I think I'll just give her a little kiss.

PISTHETAIROS: No, you fool! Look at her beak— you'd never be the same again.

EUELPIDES: Nonsense, it's easy . . . just like shelling an egg.

He takes off the NIGHTINGALE'S *mask, and kisses her.*

See?

TEREUS: Come on, come on.

PISTHETAIROS: Lead the way, then.

They go inside, and the CHORUS *and* PROKNE (*the flautist*) *prepare for the parabasis.*

CHORUS:
Come now, my darling, come my love,
My nightingale, my turtle-dove,
Come and sing with us.
Come out, my sweet one, come and sing,
My honey-love with golden wing,
Come and play for us.

CHORUS A:
O you mortals, who, leaf-like, live only a day,
You wasters, you clay-men, who live without light,
Who are wingless and heedless, like children at play,
Though shrouded in sorrow and darkened by night;
Attend to your masters, the lords of the air.
For we'll tell you of Darkness, the Birth of the Sky,
And of Chaos and Blackness, and Doom in its lair.
First there was Chaos, and Dark like the tomb—
Neither Heaven, nor Sky, nor the Earth had been born.
And in darkness, in silence, in Night's secret womb
A black egg was conceived in a waste-land forlorn.
As the seasons passed by, in the egg Love awoke,
The gleaming, the golden, the wind-winged, the bright.
And from Love and from Darkness, grey-coiling like smoke,

The birds were the first-born, the children of Night.
We were children of Love; after us came the sky,
And the earth, and the gods, and the wide wasted ocean.
We came first; we're your rulers; we watch from on high
And guide you through life with paternal devotion.
We tell you the seasons: when the crane's on the wing,
For the farmer it's seed-time, for sailors a rest;
The kite's reappearance sheep-shearing will bring,
And the swallow advises you: "Buy a thick vest!"
Go to Ammon or Delphi, Dodona or Crete;
The birds will advise you as well as the priests,
What to buy, when to sell, what invest in or eat,
Whom to marry, whom ask out to dinners and feasts ...

CHORUS B:

Yes, the birds are your friends,
Not aloof like the gods.
Zeus up there never bends,
Never dozes or nods.
We don't hide in the sky
With a snooty expression,
And none of us try
To encourage depression!
We're always on hand
To do good to you all—
To bring off what you plan,
To be near when you call.
Peace, happiness, wealth,
Good fortune, long life,
Laughing children, good health,
An adoring, sweet wife—
All these, and still more,
Will be yours, if you just
Spurn the gods, and adore

28

Us, the friends you can trust!

CHORUS:
Muse of the woodland glade,
Fair lady, who in the forest's shade
Share with us your heavenly note,
Uttered forth from golden throat,
Sing with us now; sing hymns to Pan,
Raise up the strains that mortal man
Can never echo—sweet one, sing
Till your voice makes all the woodlands ring.

There is a short flute interlude, and then CHORUS C *steps forward.*

CHORUS C:
Ladies and gentlemen, you know the life we lead.
If any of you have ever felt the need
For a quiet life, come up and join us now.
You're vexed and harassed by the law; you bow
To it because you have to—here, we're free.
"It's wrong to beat your father"—here, you'll see,
A fighting cock is proud to fight his son.
With us, fear's no shame for anyone:
We've running birds, and ducks, and quails galore!
And if you want a higher rank than before,
Come and join us—no one here's a slave,
No one's poor, no one's anything but brave.

CHORUS:
Just as in rippling lakes,
By the bank, where the ripple breaks,
The once-mute swans begin to sing,
And in the forest every living thing
Cowers down and listens, hushed with fright;
So let our song rise to the light,

29

Till Olympos itself resounds, its lords
Enraptured, awe-struck by our words.
CHORUS C:
There's nothing more useful than a pair of wings.
Suppose you're at a play, and the theatre rings
With hammy acting, or your stomach rumbles—
Fly off, go home, have breakfast, end your grumbles,
And when that actor's finished, fly right back!
If you're in dire distress, really on the rack,
No need to sit there steaming . . . or suppose
You fancy someone else's wife? The show's
Begun; you see her husband in the theatre;
Fly off, have fun, come back—what could be neater?
I tell you, whatever needs you have, all things
Are easier for those of us with wings!

SCENE TWO

As the CHORUS finish, PISTHETAIROS, EUEL-
PIDES and TEREUS come out. The two Athenians have
now got wings.

PISTHETAIROS: Well, there you are, then! My god,
I've never seen anything funnier!

EUELPIDES offended: What's so funny?

PISTHETAIROS: Your wings! D'you know what you
look like? A plaster duck on the bathroom wall!

EUELPIDES: I'd rather look like a plaster duck than a
half-witted blackbird! Come on, what's next?

PISTHETAIROS: We'd better find a name for the city—
something long and sonorous, that'll really impress people.

EUELPIDES: What about Sparta?

PISTHETAIROS: Good heavens! Isn't one Sparta bad
enough?

EUELPIDES: It's always impressed me.

TEREUS: It ought to have a cuckoo in it somewhere . . . and clouds . . .

PISTHETAIROS: I know. Cloudcuckooborough!

TEREUS: You've got it . . . Cloudcuckooborough!

EUELPIDES: Yes, Cloudcuckooborough, where all the castles in the air are built.

PISTHETAIROS: Right, fly up and give the builders a hand . . . you know, carrying bricks, mixing cement, falling off ladders, drawing water, setting guards, damping down the watchfires, inspecting the watchmen, sleeping on the job . . . Oh, and send off a couple of messengers. One to the gods, and one down to earth. Tell them to report back to me—they must see me personally.

EUELPIDES *irritably*: See you personally in hell, I hope!

PISTHETAIROS: Go on, don't argue. (*wheedling*) There's no one else I can trust to do it properly. I've got to stay here, and sacrifice to our new gods. Go on . . .

    EUELPIDES *goes out grumbling*.

Now, where's the priest? Boy! Bring me the basket and the water-jug.

Suddenly there is the sound of a hymn off. The PRIEST *comes into view, accompanied by a breathy and inefficient flautist dressed in black. The priest is singing in a raucous but holy voice, full of fervour:*

PRIEST:
    Here's a scheme to please us all,
    Quite a brilliant plan;
    I'll be ready when you call,
    I'm the very man.
    First we'll sacrifice a sheep:
    That will please the crowd.

Chairis' flute the time will keep,
Blowing long and loud . . .

Onward to the sa-hacrifice—

PISTHETAIROS: Stop, stop, for heaven's sake! I don't
believe it: a *crow* . . . playing the flute? What a couple!

PRIEST *huffily*: There's no need to be rude.

PISTHETAIROS: All right, all right. Get on with the
sacrifice.

PRIEST: Very well. Bring me the basket. Ready? (*chanting*) "O Hestia, the hearthfire, and the holy hawk, and
the birds in heaven and the earth beneath . . ."

PISTHETAIROS *imitating the chant*: "Great eagle, lord
of Sunion . . ."

PRIEST: "O Sabazian finch, O sparrow, great mother of all
the world, prophetic swans, Apollo's hawk, great quail-
born Artemis, we beseech you all . . . keep safe Cloudcuckooborough, guard it from all ills soever . . ."

PISTHETAIROS *aside*: "Soever"? What sort of a word is
that?

PRIEST: "O hero birds, and heroes' sons, O gannets, peli-
cans, cranes, magpies, mallards, widgeons, peacocks, dippers, curlews, petrels, sparrow-hawks, vultures, kites . . ."

PISTHETAIROS: Stop, you fool! What're you inviting
vultures for? Look at the victim: one vulture, and there'll
be nothing for anyone else. Oh, clear off . . . I'll do it!

The PRIEST *begins his hymn again, desperately.*

PRIEST:
Sir, I soon can change my tune
And pray as you desire;
Any tiny little thing . . .

PISTHETAIROS: Go on, clear off!

He chases the PRIEST *away, but only as far as the*

*edge of the stage, where he waits like a hovering buzzard,
while* PISTHETAIROS *comes back to start the sacrifice
again.*

I don't know . . . (*chanting*) With this sacrifice, I pray
to all the winged gods . . .

He is interrupted by the dramatic entry of the POET.

POET *elaborately:*

"O happy spot! O Muse-hymned, happy haunt!
Elysium! Cloudcuckooborough sublime!"

PISTHETAIROS: What now? Who the devil are you?

POET: A poet, sir . . . one of nature's craftsmen . . .

PISTHETAIROS *aside:* Nature's craftsmen? Oh dear, oh
dear! (*aloud*) Well, what d'you want?

POET: I've composed an ode celebrating your city . . .
and a sonnet-sequence . . . and a limerick in the style of
Simonides: "There once was a town in the sky . . ."

PISTHETAIROS: What d'you mean, composed? When?

POET *elaborately:*

"For years long past, your city's fame
Hath filled my lips; her glorious name . . ."

PISTHETAIROS: Years long past? She's only just got
her name!

POET:

"The Muses, windswift, came
Like horses—wild or tame—
And told me. O my lord,
How easily you could afford
A little fee,
Some small reward
For reams of lyric poetry!"

PISTHETAIROS *aside:* I see!

Suddenly he advances on the PRIEST, *who backs away
in alarm.*

33

Here, you've got a jacket. Take it off, and give it to the poet here!

After a short struggle the PRIEST's *jacket is removed.*

POET:

With joyous, thankful hearts,
The Muse and I . . . er . . . departs . . .

PISTHETAIROS: Thank goodness!

POET *inexorably:*

No longer must we roam
Forlorn and far from home;
Though, for fine verse like this,
A . . . *coat* . . . wouldn't come amiss . . .

PISTHETAIROS: Well, you heard him. He wants your coat as well.

He takes the PRIEST's *coat and gives it to the* POET.

PRIEST *shivering and chanting:* I call on almighty Zeus to destroy this city and all its works, and especially Pisthetairos . . .

PISTHETAIROS: What? Destroy me, eh? Clear off! Shoo!

PRIEST ⎫
⎬ *simultaneously* ⎧ Destroy him utterly, both root and branch . . .
POET ⎭ ⎩ Haunt of the birds, home of the heavenly ones . . .

PISTHETAIROS: Go on . . . get out!

He shoos them out, still chanting and singing.

News of the city certainly got around fast . . . Ah well, I suppose I'd better finish the sacrifice. Pick up the holy water, and walk round the altar . . .

The PROPHET *rushes in, clutching a huge book of oracles.*

PROPHET: Stop! Don't sacrifice that animal!

34

PISTHETAIROS: Don't sacrifice . . . ? Who on earth are *you*?

PROPHET: I'm a prophet.

PISTHETAIROS: Oh, hard *luck* . . . we don't need any prophets today . . .

PROPHET: What? Are you crazy? You can't sacrifice without a prophet. Don't you know there's an oracle of Lord Bakis expressly referring to Cloudcuckooborough?

PISTHETAIROS: There is, is there? And why didn't you say so before?

PROPHET: You didn't ask me, did you?

PISTHETAIROS: But the city was only founded five minutes ago.

PROPHET: Lord Bakis knows neither time nor place.

PISTHETAIROS: Oh, all right. Get on with it.

PROPHET:
> Lord Bakis decrees, when a wolf and a white-headed raven
> Inhabit together the space betwixt Sicyon and Corinth . . .

PISTHETAIROS: Corinth? What's Corinth got to do with it?

PROPHET *pityingly*: By "Corinth" he means the air, of course! Listen . . .
> "When this comes about, first offer Pandora a ram;
> And present to whoever comes first to interpret my sayings
> A cloak, clean and new, and a new pair of sandals . . ."

PISTHETAIROS: Sandals? He really said sandals?

PROPHET: Here, it's in the book . . . read it for yourself.
> ". . . and a jar full of wine, and a share of the entrails."

PISTHETAIROS: That's all in there?

PROPHET: Look for yourself.

35

PISTHETAIROS: But this oracle is quite different from the one I had from Apollo:

"A beggar, unsummoned, will try to share your feasting,
Disturb your sacrifice, greedy for most of the entrails;
Beat him and kick him and smash in his rib-cage!"

PROPHET *nervously*: That's nonsense!

PISTHETAIROS: Here, it's in the book. Look for yourself . . .

He hits him with the book.

Now, get out, will you?

PROPHET: Ow, ow! All right, I'm going!

PISTHETAIROS: Peddle your oracles somewhere else!

He chases him out, as METON, *a mathematician, enters.*

METON: I have come amongst you . . .

PISTHETAIROS: Oh god, not another one. What do *you* want?

METON: I've come to take precise measurements of your atmosphere, to make an accurate surveyance, and get it properly allocated, according to genuine mathematical principles, as laid down by . . .

PISTHETAIROS: For heaven's sake! Who *are* you?

METON: Meton . . . astronomer, mathematician and geographer extraordinary, *at* your service.

He takes out a gigantic pair of compasses.

PISTHETAIROS: Ow! What are those for?

METON: They're compasses for measuring the air. It's hollow, d'you see, like a tube . . . I stick one end in down here, and turn the other end round about, until I find the radius of the diameter . . . is that clear?

PISTHETAIROS *sarcastically*: Clear?

METON: Good. Then I straighten it up, and take the square area of the circle heretofore formed . . . that's your

36

market-place, as will be, with roads going off at tangents here and here, like the rays of the sun. . . .

PISTHETAIROS: Pythagoras walks again! Hey, Meton.

METON: Yes?

PISTHETAIROS: Let me give you some advice.

METON: Advice?

PISTHETAIROS: Yes: clear off!

METON: Why?

PISTHETAIROS: The birds hate strangers. If they catch you here . . .

METON: What d'you mean? Are they having a revolution?

PISTHETAIROS: Not exactly.

METON: What then?

PISTHETAIROS: They just hate beggars.

METON *offended*: Oh, in that case . . . I'll go . . .

PISTHETAIROS: I would if I were you. (*suddenly*) Look out, they're coming!

METON: Help!

He rushes out.

PISTHETAIROS: That's right . . . go and measure yourself somewhere else!

An AMBASSADOR *in full rig-out comes in.*

AMBASSADOR: Where's the welcoming committee?

PISTHETAIROS: Good heavens, a walking tailor's shop!

AMBASSADOR: I am your ambassador . . .

PISTHETAIROS: Who from?

AMBASSADOR: The Athenians. I have full authority . . .

PISTHETAIROS: . . . to make a nuisance of yourself! All right, I'll give you a year's salary—go home and make a nuisance there.

AMBASSADOR: With pleasure. I was halfway through

37

an important piece of legislation when I had to leave. A motion before the Assembly . . .

PISTHETAIROS: Here, then. Here's your salary.

He hits him.

AMBASSADOR: Ow! What's that?

PISTHETAIROS *gesturing to the audience*: A motion before the Assembly. And here's the seconder . . .

He hits him again.

AMBASSADOR: You can't do that . . . I've got diplomatic immunity.

PISTHETAIROS: And that's just where I'll hit you if you don't clear off! (To *the audience*) Fantastic: they send an ambassador, and we haven't even sacrificed!

The BARRISTER *comes in, a roll of laws under one arm.*

BARRISTER *reading from his laws*: "If any Cloudcuckooburgher wrongs a man of Athens . . ."

PISTHETAIROS: Oh no! Not another one!

BARRISTER: I've brought you a constitution . . . brand-new laws, latest model . . .

PISTHETAIROS: Give me an example.

BARRISTER *reading*: "Cloudcuckooburghers will use the weights and measures of the Olophyxians . . ."

PISTHETAIROS: Olophyxians? Ollo-fix-*you* if you don't clear off!

BARRISTER: What's the matter?

PISTHETAIROS: Out! Take your laws and . . . just a minute, here's a law for you!

He starts beating him.

AMBASSADOR: I summons Pisthetairos for assault and battery.

PISTHETAIROS: Oh, do you? Here's some more, then!

BARRISTER *reading*: "If anyone illtreats an officer of state . . ."

PISTHETAIROS: Get out! Shoo!

AMBASSADOR: I'll see you in court! Ten thousand gold pieces, at least . . . I'll show you!

PISTHETAIROS: Get out, before I kick your lawbox in!

BARRISTER: Do you remember the 19th inst, the night you peed against . . .

PISTHETAIROS: Out, out, the pair of you! Oh, it's no use: I'll have to sacrifice inside!

He goes inside and slams the door. The CHORUS *appear, and the* AMBASSADOR *and* BARRISTER *leave together, planning their revenge.*

CHORUS:
How happy are the birds! We live
A life of ease, untouched
By the miseries of mortal men.
The sun does not burn us in summer,
And in winter our feathers protect us
From icy winds and chilling frosts.
All summer long, while crickets,
Drunk with sunlight, chirp the days away,
We live in flowery meadows
And build our homes in leafy valleys;
In winter the Nymphs invite us
To share their caves in the mountain-side—
We feast with them there
On endless banquets of myrtle-berries
Gathered from the larders of the gods.

CHORUS A:
The birds are all-seeing, all-powerful, the kings
Of the air and the rulers of men.

CHORUS B:
    With justice the universe rings
    With our praise: over marsh, field and fen
    We pick off and destroy all the pests
    That devour the soft buds, or kill trees
    With their cancerous, hollowed-out nests.
CHORUS C:
    We keep watch with a dexterous ease
    On your gardens; from high overhead
    We swoop down on the danger below—
    Snakes, locusts and slugs are all dead
    Before they can harm you. You owe
    To the birds all a good harvest sends:
CHORUS A:
    Bow down, then, and worship us—birds are your
        friends!

    *They dance to the accompaniment of a flute. As they
    finish,* PISTHETAIROS *comes out again, rubbing his
    hands.*

PISTHETAIROS: Well, that's the sacrifice finished. No
    word from the wall yet? I wonder how they're getting on?
EUELPIDES *off, breathlessly:* Wh-wh-where's Pisthetai-
    ros?
PISTHETAIROS: What now?

    EUELPIDES *rushes in, out of breath.*

EUELPIDES: *Oh, aah, ohh* . . . Pisthetairos . . . *ooh,
    aargh* . . . where are you?
PISTHETAIROS: Here.
EUELPIDES: The wall's . . . *hoo, aargh* . . . finished.
PISTHETAIROS: Marvellous!
EUELPIDES: *Hoo, haa, hoo* . . . a beautiful piece of
    work . . . wide enough for four horses to gallop round

. . . *haaargh*!

PISTHETAIROS: Heavens!

EUELPIDES: And it's over a hundred yards high. I measured it . . . *phoo-hey!* . . . myself.

PISTHETAIROS: Good lord! Whoever built it that size?

EUELPIDES: The birds. No navvies, no Egyptian pyramid-builders . . . just the birds. Thirty thousand Libyan cranes flew in with cropfuls of stones, and handed them over to stonebills for cornering. There were sand-martens to mix cement, and hundreds of river birds to keep the supply of water constant.

PISTHETAIROS: What about the fetching and carrying?

EUELPIDES: *Carrion* crows, of course! It was an incredible sight: a duck-chain passing bricks along, beak to beak . . . swallows darting about like apprentices, carrying cement . . .

PISTHETAIROS: Who did the carpentering?

EUELPIDES: Woodpeckers, pecking out the gates. The *noise* . . . it was worse than a shipyard! Everything's ready now: gates closed, watch set, beacons lit, tours of inspection toured, wall closed for the day . . . Well, excuse me: I'm going to have a bath.

He goes in.

PISTHETAIROS: That was quick work. Everything finished already . . .

WATCHMAN *off*: To arms! To arms!

PISTHETAIROS: Who's this now? Does it never end?

The WATCHMAN *rushes in.*

WATCHMAN: To arms! To arms! Oh dear, oh dear . . . to arms!

PISTHETAIROS: What's wrong?

WATCHMAN: The wall's been breached . . . a mes-

41

senger from Zeus broke through the gates, slipped past the guards . . .

PISTHETAIROS *annoyed:* Who was it?

WATCHMAN: No idea . . . it had wings, that's all we know.

PISTHETAIROS: Where are the security guards? We ought to send out a posse . . .

WATCHMAN: We have already. Three thousand archer-hawks, a squadron of falcons, ospreys, eagles and vultures —he won't escape, whoever he is.

PISTHETAIROS: What about slingers and bowmen? Send the captains to me. And someone fetch me a sling!

CHORUS *excitedly:*
War, war, war is begun;
Keep a close watch, everyone—
Don't let a single god get through,
Be careful: they're at war with *you*!

CHORUS A: Look out . . . there's something coming!

IRIS *flies in, fiercely.*

PISTHETAIROS: Hey, hey, where are you going? Calm down! Steady, steady! Who are you, anyway? And where are you from?

IRIS *briefly:* Olympos.

PISTHETAIROS *pointing to her helmet:* But who are you? What are you—a warrior or a watering-can?

IRIS: I'm Iris the Swift.

PISTHETAIROS: Who?

IRIS: The messenger of the gods.

PISTHETAIROS: Quick, someone: arrest her!

IRIS: Arrest me? Don't you know . . . ?

PISTHETAIROS: Yes, I know . . . it's not going to be pleasant . . .

IRIS: What d'you mean? Have you gone raving mad?

PISTHETAIROS: Which gate did you fly through?

IRIS: Gate? I didn't see any gate.

PISTHETAIROS: Hah! Listen to that! Didn't see any gate! Have you a permit? Did you get a visa from the chief Crow?

IRIS: You're crazy!

PISTHETAIROS: I knew it . . . no visa, passport not in order . . .

IRIS: Passport? No one gave me a passport.

PISTHETAIROS: There you are, then. Illegal entry! You violate someone else's air-space . . .

IRIS: Look here, I *am* an immortal god, you know.

PISTHETAIROS: That's no excuse.

IRIS: We can fly wherever we like.

PISTHETAIROS: Not here, you can't. You're in real trouble . . . illegal entry, trespassing, evading arrest. Death's the least you can expect.

IRIS: But I'm *immortal*!

PISTHETAIROS: Don't think that'll save you. It would be a poor sort of state that let just *anybody* fly across its borders and violate its frontiers, just because they were immortal gods!

IRIS *starts to flap her wings.*

Hey! Where are you going?

IRIS *impatiently*: I can't stand here all day. I'm taking a message from Zeus down to earth: they've got to step up their sacrifices a bit. The Powers on High are getting peckish.

PISTHETAIROS: Powers on high? Who do you mean?

IRIS: Us, of course! The gods.

PISTHETAIROS: *You*, gods?

43

IRIS: Who else?

PISTHETAIROS: Ah! I see you haven't heard. We're their gods now: the birds, not Zeus.

IRIS *furiously*:

"Thou fool! Beware! Great thund'ring Jove
Will blast thee if thou utter'st more!
Thy home and self he'll quite destroy,
And leave thee crushéd to the dust!"

PISTHETAIROS: Listen to her! What pantomime did that come from? D'you think I'm scared by that sort of rubbish? You listen to me:

"If Zeus doth dare to rouse my wrath,
I'll dash him down with eagle-fire;
I'll send a flock of birds aloft
To burn his palace! Tell thy sire!"

And as for you, young lady: if you annoy me any more, I'll take you inside and show you my credentials.

IRIS: You filthy old man!

PISTHETAIROS: Go on, fly away. Shoo!

IRIS: I'll tell my father!

PISTHETAIROS: Huh! Find someone younger to frighten. Clear off! Shoo!

He shoos her out like a tame pigeon.

CHORUS:

The Olympian gods, by our decree,
Must to this town all strangers be;
No smoke from earthly sacrifice
Must pass through, or to heaven rise.

PISTHETAIROS: I wonder where the messenger's got to,
. . . the one we sent down to earth?

The MESSENGER *rushes in, very excitedly.*

MESSENGER: Pisthetairos! Oh happy man, oh blessed

saviour! Oh wisest, most brilliant, most transparently clever! Oh happy man, oh for goodness sake ask me what I want!

PISTHETAIROS: What is it?

MESSENGER: It's men, down there. They want to give you a golden crown, and decorate you for your services to mankind.

PISTHETAIROS: That's very nice. But why?

MESSENGER: Sir, you should just see them! They're all clamouring to come and join your city. Being birds is the latest craze: they leap out of bed with the lark, and fly into court; then they perch on their law-books, and chirp and twitter at their judgements. All their songs are about birds nowadays: they're always "swinging the swallow" or "howling the owl"—and as for "O for the wings of a dove" . . . ! I tell you, you'd better get a stock of wings in . . . there are hundreds of people coming up here to join your colony!

PISTHETAIROS: Good lord! Euelpides! Fetch all the baskets you can, and fill them with wings. Quickly! Bring them out here . . . I'll wait to welcome the visitors!

As the MESSENGER leaves, the CHORUS begin an excited bustle. PISTHETAIROS is too annoyed by the non-appearance of the wings to notice the discrepancy between their song and what he is saying.

CHORUS:
  Soon this city full will be
  Of men who've come to live with me . . .

PISTHETAIROS: Yes, you could be right.

CHORUS:
  What joy to share our feathered city . . .

PISTHETAIROS: Where are those wings?

CHORUS:

    With all that's wise and good and pretty.

    The only place where smiling Peace

    Rules men, where Love will never cease.

PISTHETAIROS: Oh come on! Where are they?

CHORUS:

    See! Men will come in dense array,

    Longing to live the birds' new way . . .

PISTHETAIROS: What are you doing in there?

CHORUS:

    An ideal state, from anger free:

    Where love is king, all men agree . . .

PISTHETAIROS: You really are hopeless!

    EUELPIDES *staggers out with some heavy baskets of wings. Singing off:*

BOY *off*: I want to be an eagle! I want to fly, free as the air . . .

PISTHETAIROS: I thought you were never coming! Put them down, then. Be quick . . . they're on their way!

    The WARLIKE BOY *comes in.*

BOY: There's nothing I want more than wings. I want to fly . . . I want to be a bird; I want to live here, and share your laws . . .

PISTHETAIROS: Which laws? We've got a lot of laws.

BOY: All of them . . . but especially the one that says a son can beat his father.

PISTHETAIROS: Oh yes: it's perfectly natural up here for a fighting cock to challenge his father to a duel.

BOY: That's really why I've come: I want to get rid of my father and inherit all his money.

PISTHETAIROS: H'm. But we've got another law, that

46

when a father crane is old and weary, and has worn himself out bringing up his cranelets, the young birds must take over, and look after *him*.

BOY: Look *after* him? Don't tell me I've come to the wrong place . . .

PISTHETAIROS: No, no, I've got an idea. Since you're so keen to be a bird, take these wings and this cockspur, and go and join our fighter squadron. Let your father live in peace—we'll find you enough fighting to keep you happy.

BOY: Mmm . . . that doesn't sound a bad idea. All right!

PISTHETAIROS: Good! Off you go, then.

The BOY *goes out, and* KINESIAS *the lyric poet makes his entry. He is a tall pansyish creature with a lisp.*

KINESIAS:
    "White-pinioned, I wend to heaven my flighty way,
    Thong-thwung o'er the myriad paths of melody . . ."

PISTHETAIROS: It's Kinesias! What'th bwought you here, my fwiend?

KINESIAS:
    "I wish to be a bird . . . a liquid nightingale!"

PISTHETAIROS: For goodness sake stop singing! What is it you want?

KINESIAS: I want you to give me wingth, tho that I can flit about from cloud to cloud, picking up inthpiration for my withpy, heavenly odeth.

PISTHETAIROS: Odeth? I mean odes? From the sky?

KINESIAS: Yeth. They hang there like orangeth, jutht waiting to be gathered. You know the thort of thing we poetth write about: dark-thcudding, thky-rathing, fleeth-whitening . . . I'll give you an example . . .

PISTHETAIROS *hastily*: No, no, it's all right . . .

47

KINESIAS: I thought you'd like that.

He clears his throat.

Harrumph! Haaaaarumph! "On airy flight: an ode in fifty vertheth."

"Wing-shadowth, airy-flight,
Thoft-feathered, bird invethted . . ."

PISTHETAIROS *aside:* Oh dear!

KINESIAS:

". . . high-flying, thtorm-totththing,
Wind-riven, breath-blown,
Wing-beaten, earth-cleaving . . ."

PISTHETAIROS *suddenly hits him with a pair of wings.*

Ow! What wath that for?

PISTHETAIROS: I thought you wanted to be wing-beaten.

KINESIAS: You're laughing at me . . . *me*, the leading lyrithitht in Greethe! People fight to hear me rethite.

PISTHETAIROS: Well, why not stay? People will fight *here* when you recite . . . fight to get away!

KINESIAS: I'm not thtaying here to be inthulted. But I warn you: I won't be thatithfied until I can fly, and thircumnavigate the heaventh . . .

He goes out grumbling.

PISTHETAIROS: Well, good riddanth, that's all I can say.

The INFORMER *comes in.*

INFORMER: The swallows . . . where are the swallows? I must see the swallows?

PISTHETAIROS: Seeing swallows? You're in a bad way.

INFORMER: Where's the man who's issuing wings?

PISTHETAIROS: Here. What d'you want?

48

INFORMER: Wings, of course.

PISTHETAIROS: Why?

INFORMER: My job. I go round the islands, picking up information, serving writs and summonses, and acting as bailiff . . .

PISTHETAIROS: A real public benefactor!

INFORMER: The straits round the islands are full of pirates, who make my job very difficult. With wings, and a flock of cranes to escort me, I could flit in and out with a cropful of summonses, and save myself a lot of trouble.

PISTHETAIROS: So that's your job . . . at your age? You spend your time spying on other people?

INFORMER: What else can I do? Dig up roads?

PISTHETAIROS: Surely there are other honest jobs you could do, without informing.

INFORMER: Look, it's wings I came for, not a sermon.

PISTHETAIROS: My advice'll give you wings.

INFORMER: What's that supposed to mean?

PISTHETAIROS: Words are wings.

INFORMER: What?

PISTHETAIROS: All men use words to wing themselves: you know how people talk—"Dietrephes has so inspired my son with his talk of horses that the boy's flown off to learn to drive" . . . or, "My boy's got very flighty lately: buries his head in the clouds, reads nothing but poetry . . ."

INFORMER: I don't know what you're talking about.

PISTHETAIROS: Simple: words inspire the mind to flights of fancy. I was hoping my words would inspire *you* to an honest job of work.

INFORMER: But I don't want an honest job of work.

PISTHETAIROS: What?

INFORMER: Informing's in my blood . . . father, grand-father before him. I can't disgrace my family. Come on,

49

stop wasting time. Give me some wings—hawk's or falcon's, I'm not fussy—so that I can fly out and deliver the islanders their summonses. You've got to move fast in my job: faster than a whipping-top, in fact.

PISTHETAIROS: A whipping-top, eh? H'mm . . . I think I can oblige you. Here!

He begins whipping him.

INFORMER: What's this? A whip?

PISTHETAIROS: No, no: wings! Wings to make you into a whipping-top!

INFORMER: Ow! Ow!

PISTHETAIROS: There, whip off somewhere else! Go on: you'll get nothing out of me. Clear off!

He whips him out, then goes back to EUELPIDES.

Here, these wings are in a terrible mess. Help sort them out, will you?

As he and EUELPIDES *start sorting the wings, a dark figure creeps in, with only his eyes visible above the edge of his cloak . . .* PROMETHEUS.

PROMETHEUS: Oh dear, oh dear, I do hope Zeus doesn't see me! Psst! Where's Pisthetairos?

PISTHETAIROS: Here. Good heavens, who's this walking mystery?

PROMETHEUS: Shhh! Listen: are there any gods about?

PISTHETAIROS: Not that I can see. Who are you?

PROMETHEUS: Shhh! What time is it?

PISTHETAIROS: Oh . . . er . . . a little after noon. Who *are* you?

PROMETHEUS: Shhh! How long after? What's Zeus doing? Is it dark, or sunny?

PISTHETAIROS *losing his patience*: Oh dear, oh dear!

PROMETHEUS: All clear? In that case, I'll come out.

He unwraps himself.

PISTHETAIROS *delighted*: Prometheus!

PROMETHEUS: Shhhhh! For heaven's sake, not so loud.

PISTHETAIROS: What's the matter?

PROMETHEUS: Don't shout my name all over the place. If Zeus gets to know I'm here . . . I've come down to tell you what's going on in heaven. Look, hold up this umbrella, so the gods can't see me.

They put up a huge umbrella.

PISTHETAIROS: Brilliant! Here, come underneath . . . Now, what have you got to tell me?

PROMETHEUS: Listen . . .

PISTHETAIROS: I'm listening.

PROMETHEUS *looks all round, then whispers confidentially:*

PROMETHEUS: Zeus is done for.

PISTHETAIROS: Done for? When?

PROMETHEUS: When you closed the middle air. No one's sacrificing to the gods any more . . . we haven't had a sniff of offering all day. Everyone's on emergency rations. It's all right for the Greek gods . . . they know how to take it. But some of the foreigners are turning a bit nasty . . . saying they'll finish Zeus off if he doesn't reopen the trade-routes and let the sacrifices through again.

PISTHETAIROS: You mean there are other gods, as well as Greek ones?

PROMETHEUS: Heavens, yes. Funny lot too, if you ask me.

PISTHETAIROS: What are they called?

PROMETHEUS: Triballians.

PISTHETAIROS *laughing*: Triballians? That explains everything.

51

PROMETHEUS: I'm telling you, there's going to be trouble. They're sending down negotiators, from Zeus and the Triballians, to ask for a truce. But if you take my advice, you'll hold out till Zeus lets you marry Queenie.

PISTHETAIROS: Queenie? Who's she?

PROMETHEUS: A very nice young goddess, believe me . . . polishes Zeus's thunderbolts, and looks after everything: councils, laws, good sense, shipping, freedom of speech, fair play for jurors—the lot!

PISTHETAIROS: All that?

PROMETHEUS: Yes. Marry her, and you've got everything. Anyway, that's my advice. You know I've always been on the side of men.

PISTHETAIROS: The god who brought us fire.

PROMETHEUS: Yes—and that didn't do me any good with *them*, I can tell you. Look, I've got to go. Take the umbrella, will you, and walk in front. That way, if Zeus does see me, he'll think I'm part of a procession.

PISTHETAIROS: All right. Here: carry this deckchair . . . that'll make it look more natural.

They process inside, as the deputation from Heaven, POSEIDON, HERAKLES *and a* TRIBALLIAN GOD, *come in.*

POSEIDON: Here we are . . . Cloudcuckooborough. Fancy, *us*, ambassadors to a place like this! (*To the* TRIBALLIAN) For goodness sake put your cloak straight . . . over the other shoulder! What a specimen! Why we ever brought him with us . . .

He starts pulling at the TRIBALLIAN's *cloak.*

TRIBALLIAN *fiercely*: Hands off!

POSEIDON: I've never seen a more unpleasant specimen! Here, Herakles, have you got it straight yet? What's our

52

plan of campaign?

HERAKLES: Find out who built the wall, and throttle him.

POSEIDON: No, no . . . we're supposed to be a *peace* mission!

HERAKLES: All right . . . we make peace, and then throttle him.

PISTHETAIROS *comes out, followed by* EUEL-PIDES *with a kitchen table. They begin cooking, pretending not to notice the gods.* HERAKLES, *a proverbial glutton, is very interested in the preparations.*

PISTHETAIROS: Bring me the cheese-grater. Where's the garlic? I can't find the cheese. Blow up the fire for me.

POSEIDON: Haarumph! The Heavenly Embassy presents its credentials to this mortal man.

PISTHETAIROS: Just a minute while I chop the garlic.

HERAKLES: Hey! What sort of meat is this?

PISTHETAIROS: Hands off! Some traitors, caught plotting against the state.

HERAKLES: You pluck them and cook them in garlic, then?

PISTHETAIROS: Herakles! How nice to see you!

POSEIDON: Ahem! The peace-mission from Heaven presents its credentials . . .

PISTHETAIROS: We're running out of cooking-oil.

HERAKLES: Oh no! Birds need plenty of oil.

POSEIDON *desperately*: We didn't start the war . . . and we certainly aren't benefiting from it. On the other hand, *you* could benefit from peace: we'll make sure your water tanks are never empty, and see to it that you always have fine weather. We've full authority . . .

PISTHETAIROS: Well, we didn't start the war, either

—and we're quite prepared to grant peace, if you give us our rights.

POSEIDON: Rights?

PISTHETAIROS: Yes. Give back the birds their former power and sovereignty. If we're agreed on that, I invite the ambassadors to dinner.

HERAKLES *eagerly*: Agreed! Agreed! That seems quite fair to me!

POSEIDON: You fool! You always put your stomach before your head! Would you like to see your own father Zeus deprived of his power?

PISTHETAIROS: No, no, you don't understand. Let the birds rule down here, and you gods will be better off than ever before. You know the trouble you've always had because of the clouds: you can't see men half the time, skulking away underneath them, mocking you, taking your names in vain. Well, if you get the birds on your side, whenever someone curses by Zeus, a crow will fly straight down and poke his eye out.

POSEIDON: By Poseidon, that's rather clever.

HERAKLES: I agree.

POSEIDON *to the* TRIBALLIAN: What about you?

TRIBALLIAN *shrugging*: Sinoffeta.

PISTHETAIROS: You see, he agrees. And there's something else we can do for you. Suppose a mortal makes a promise—"Grant this wish, and I'll sacrifice you a sheep" —then delays, thinking: "The gods are immortal; they can wait!" . . . we'll deal with him for you.

POSEIDON: How?

PISTHETAIROS: We'll wait till he's counting his money, or having a bath, then send a kite down to pick off two of his fattest sheep, as a present for the gods.

HERAKLES *excitedly*: Two sheep? Give them back their

54

crown, I say!

POSEIDON: What about Triballos?

HERAKLES *to* TRIBALLOS, *showing his fist*: You agree, don't you?

TRIBALLIAN: Ree, ree!

HERAKLES: There you are . . . democracy in action.

POSEIDON: All right, I know when I'm beaten. I agree.

They turn back to PISTHETAIROS.

HERAKLES: Very well, we'll give it back.

PISTHETAIROS: Just a moment, just a moment. There's one thing I nearly forgot. I don't want Hera . . . Zeus can keep her . . . but you must hand Queenie over to me.

POSEIDON: Impossible! It's obvious you don't want to make peace at all! Come on, you two . . .

PISTHETAIROS: Oh well, it's all the same to me. All I'm worried about is whether this sauce is sweet enough.

HERAKLES *is suddenly struck by what he is going to miss.*

HERAKLES *aside:* Eh? Sauce? (to POSEIDON) Hey! We're surely not going to argue over one little woman . . . ?

POSEIDON: What else would you suggest?

HERAKLES: Make peace, of course!

POSEIDON: Make peace? You're crazy! What's going to happen to *you* when your father Zeus hands over his power to these people? *Your* inheritance!

HERAKLES *doubtfully:* I hadn't thought of that . . .

PISTHETAIROS: Psst, Herakles! Come over here a minute . . . He's tricking you, you know. What makes you think you'd get a penny anyway? How can you? A son can't inherit till his father dies . . . and Zeus is immortal!

55

HERAKLES: I hadn't thought of that either . . .

PISTHETAIROS: But stay with us, and you're made! Captain of Fighting Birds . . . all your comforts . . . three square meals a day . . .

HERAKLES: Aha! That settles it! (*in a loud voice*) I agreed with you before, and I say again: hand her over.

PISTHETAIROS: Poseidon?

POSEIDON: Never!

PISTHETAIROS: So it's up to Triballos . . . he's got the casting vote. Well . . . what do you say?

TRIBALLOS: Queenie-birdie-handle-over. *Heap!*

HERAKLES: Hand her over, he says.

POSEIDON *furiously*: No he doesn't! He knows nothing about it!

PISTHETAIROS: Sorry: he says hand her over to the birds.

POSEIDON *sulkily*: All right, settle it yourselves. I'm having nothing to do with it.

HERAKLES: Right, it's up to us, then. Pisthetairos, I tell you what: Queenie's waiting for you, just round the back there . . . you go and fetch her, and I'll stay here and look after the meat for you.

POSEIDON *angrily*: Look after the meat! That's all you're fit for!

HERAKLES: Who's complaining?

PISTHETAIROS: Someone fetch my wedding-suit! Just round the back here? I won't be two minutes!

He goes out. Everyone else prepares for the finale. There is a loud, dramatic fanfare, and EUELPIDES *steps forward.*

EUELPIDES: Ahem! Haaaaarumph!
"Oh happy ones, oh famous, noble race,
Oh winged ones, receive your king:

56

Behold—he comes to claim his rightful place,
The golden one, the star-bright, wide of wing.
He comes, and at his side, his shining queen,
Heaven's fairest lady, bearing in her hand
Lord Zeus's thunderbolt, dread to be seen.
Awake, and welcome them into your land.
Sweet incense burn; play music loud and long;
He comes! Begin the sacred wedding song!"

The CHORUS *begin a wedding song, and slowly a
procession comes into view. In the centre* PISTHE-
TAIROS *and* QUEENIE *are carried aloft.*

CHORUS:

Draw back, give way, stand clear!
Our king is coming near!
Fly round his head with pride
And hymn his lovely bride!
Hymen-hymenai-oh.

CHORUS A:

Oh happy man, oh saviour-king,
With loving pride your praise we sing.

CHORUS:

Hymen-hymenai-oh.

CHORUS B:

Like you, great Zeus, with equal pride,
Led home his fair immortal bride.

CHORUS:

Hymen-hymenai-oh.

CHORUS C:

Young Cupid, golden-winged and fair,
With blessings showered the heavenly pair.

CHORUS:

Hymen-hymenai-oh,
Hymen-hymenai-oh.

PISTHETAIROS:

Your wedding-song is pleasing; sweet your voices.
But now, while heaven with earth rejoices,
Call up for me great Zeus's thunder . . . call
It forth, and let it for our wedding roll.

CHORUS A:

Golden thunder, heaven cleaving,
Echoed from the sea-swell's heaving,
Rise, and fright the quivering earth!
Great Zeus, lord of the upper air,
In honour of this bridal pair,
Now give your royal thunder birth!

After a short pause, there is a prolonged roll of thunder.

CHORUS:

Hymen-hymenai-oh,
Hymen-hymenai-oh.

PISTHETAIROS:

Come with us now, and follow us inside;
Birds of the air, salute my royal bride!
Come in; begin the happy ceremony
To unite us in loving matrimony.

CHORUS:

Hymen-hymenai-oh.

PISTHETAIROS:

Give me your hand, my love, and wing to wing
We'll lead the way, to end the play,
While nightingales our wedding-chorus sing.

ALL:

Hymen-hymenai-oh,
Hymen hymenai-oh.

The procession leaves. End of the play.

58

PROMETHEUS BOUND

NOTE

Aeschylus, who died in 456 B.C., was the earliest of the three great Athenian tragedians. His plays are constructed on simpler lines than those of Sophocles or Euripides: *Prometheus Bound*, for example (written some time between 470 and 460), requires only two solo actors, and contains very little of the character-drawing or elaboration of plot that we find in later plays like Sophocles' *Antigone* or Euripides' *Medea*.

Aeschylus himself, in *The Frogs*, compares his work not to the plays of other dramatists, but to the poems of Homer and Hesiod, long epics about the doings of gods, demigods and heroes. He was above all a poet, and it is for this rather than his dramatic subtlety that he is most admired today. His surviving plays are not concerned with ordinary events and people, but with great matters of good and evil, justice and injustice, acted out by Homeric heroes like Agamemnon, or the gods and demigods of *Prometheus Bound*.

This play is, in essence, a fictionalised account of the struggle for power between the older gods and the Olympians of Aeschylus' own time. Prometheus, caught between the old gods and the new, helps mankind and is punished for it. Just as in the Book of Genesis Adam and Eve are taught knowledge, and God's hopes for mankind are frustrated, so in the Prometheus legend men are given fire, and the knowledge this brings blocks Zeus's plan to create a perfect, sinless race.

It is perhaps best to regard *Prometheus Bound* more as a dramatic poem than a play. From its very opening lines, when Might and Force drag in a huge wickerwork figure of Prometheus nine or ten feet high (so that the actor could stand comfortably inside it), the audience must have realised that, even by the standards of Greek theatre, the play they were about to see would make no attempt whatever to be realistic.

PROMETHEUS BOUND

Characters in order of appearance:

MIGHT

FORCE

HEPHAISTOS, *the blacksmith god*

PROMETHEUS

OKEANOS

IO, *daughter of Inachos*

HERMES, *the messenger god*

CHORUS of *Okeanos' daughters*

PROMETHEUS BOUND

A deserted mountainside. MIGHT *and* FORCE *come in, leading* PROMETHEUS. HEPHAISTOS *follows them, carrying chains.*

MIGHT:

No further: we have come to Scythia,
The edge of the known world, a wilderness
Where no man walks. Hephaistos,
You must obey your father's orders now:
Bind Prometheus here on the mountainside,
With hard steel chains that he will never break.
It was your fire he stole, the flower and pride
Of your art: he stole it and gave it to men.
For this crime, for putting men before the gods,
He must pay the penalty, and learn
That Zeus's orders are to be obeyed.

HEPHAISTOS:

Might and Force, your part in this is over;
Now the burden is mine. For how can I fasten
My own kinsman Prometheus to this rock
And leave him in misery? Prometheus,
Noble son of Themis the counsellor,
We have both been caught up by destiny:
You must be punished, and I must punish you.
I must chain you to this bleak rock:
You will never see Man again, or hear his voice.
The sun is pitiless here: it will burn you black,
Till you scream for Night to come down and hide you.
She will come, briefly, till the next day's sun

Scatters the morning dew and renews your pain.
This is your punishment for helping men—
And no one can save you or set you free.
For you are a god, but you stole their gifts
And gave them to men—you scorned their anger
And now you must pay the price. On this rock
You will neither sleep nor rest; you must stay here,
Twisted with cramp, unable to stretch your limbs,
Until you curse the day you disobeyed.
Zeus will not give way: he is a new king.
And new kings are slow to learn the art of mercy.

MIGHT:

We are wasting time—these tears are useless.
The gods have cursed Prometheus, and you
Must hate him too. It was your fire he stole.

HEPHAISTOS:

But he is my kinsman, and I must honour him.

MIGHT:

Zeus is your father—you owe him honour too.

HEPHAISTOS:

Is there no room in your heart for pity?

MIGHT:

None. Pity is wasted on a guilty man.

HEPHAISTOS:

I curse my skill—

MIGHT:

Your skill is not to blame.
Prometheus' own crimes have earned this punishment.

HEPHAISTOS:

If only someone else—

MIGHT:

There is no one else:
These tasks are yours by right.

65

HEPHAISTOS:

I must obey?

MIGHT:

You must. Waste no more time—do it now,
Before Zeus looks down and sees you hesitating.

HEPHAISTOS:

The chains are ready.

MIGHT:

Put them on his arms.
Strike hard; fasten him firmly to the rock.

MIGHT *and* FORCE *hold* PROMETHEUS *down,
while* HEPHAISTOS *begins to chain him to the rock.*

HEPHAISTOS:

It will soon be done.

MIGHT:

Chain him securely.
He has a cunning mind—if there's a way
To free himself, he'll find it.

HEPHAISTOS:

This arm is fastened.

MIGHT:

Now this one. Our philosopher must learn
That Zeus is king of the gods, not he.

HEPHAISTOS:

There. The workmanship is perfect—
Only Prometheus will find fault with it.

MIGHT:

Now take this stake, and drive it through his chest.

HEPHAISTOS:

Prometheus, I pity you—

MIGHT:

Do you still hesitate

66

To punish Zeus's enemies? Be careful,
Or you may need all your pity for yourself.

HEPHAISTOS:
How can you look at him, and not be moved?

MIGHT:
I see nothing but a criminal being punished.
Bind his ribs firmly.

HEPHAISTOS:
                        I need no advice;
You can save your breath.

MIGHT:
                        When the job's done,
I'll save it. Go down lower: fasten his legs . . .

HEPHAISTOS:
There.

MIGHT:
            . . . and pin his ankles. Zeus will come
To inspect the work, and he is hard to please.

HEPHAISTOS:
Your tongue is like your nature: harsh.

MIGHT:
My work is harsh: I leave pity to you.

HEPHAISTOS:
It's done—he can't escape. We can go now.

MIGHT:
There, Prometheus! Now you can defy the gods;
Now you can steal their gifts and give them to men!
Will men repay you with the best gift of all—
Your freedom? Prometheus the Far-sighted,
You were wrongly named. If you had been far-sighted
You would never have earned this punishment!

MIGHT, FORCE and HEPHAISTOS go, leaving

PROMETHEUS *alone on the mountainside.*

PROMETHEUS:
O light of day, O winds on your downy wings;
Rivers, and waves of the myriad-laughing sea;
Earth, mother of all, and the Sun who smiles on them—
Look down on me now!
I am a god, and the gods have cursed me;
I must wander the endless roads of time,
Shouldering the torments Zeus has sent me
In his new-found infinite wisdom.
Weep now, as I weep, for what I am suffering
And what is still to come.
I know you, my sufferings—I have watched you
Creeping up secretly behind me,
And I know the torments that must follow you,
The inevitable slights of grim necessity.
For this is my fate, and I must bear it calmly:
I gave men a gift, and in that giving
I yoked myself to my own sure punishment.
I took a hollow reed, and filled it with fire,
The gods' most precious gift.
With fire I gave men knowledge, and an end to pain.
Their release brought my imprisonment—
I chose my own fate, and I must learn to bear it.

Shhh! What sound is that?
Who is coming? Man . . . or god . . . or demigod?
Have you come to the ends of the world to stare at me?
What do you hope to see? A god in chains,
Banished for ever from the courts of heaven,
Condemned by Zeus for loving men above the gods?

I can hear a flock of birds.

The air is alive with the beating of wings.
Whatever is coming, I fear it.

   The CHORUS *are carried in through the air in a winged chariot.*

CHORUS:
   There is nothing to fear; we are your friends.
   Far away, in deep caves under the sea,
   We heard iron ringing on iron.
   At once, barefooted, forgetting modesty,
   We set sail on the wings of the storm-winds
   And came to weep with you.
PROMETHEUS:
   Daughters of Tethys and Okeanos
   Whose sleepless tides wash the encircled earth,
   Do you see how I am suffering?
   Zeus has chained me here for ever:
   Hollow-eyed, I must keep watch on the passing years,
   And ride out the storm of the gods' displeasure.
CHORUS:
   We see you, Prometheus: we see you, and are afraid.
   We can offer nothing in your desolation
   But a cloud of empty tears.
   A new pilot is steering Olympos,
   A young king with a young king's laws;
   The glory of former days is all forgotten.
PROMETHEUS:
   If he had buried me in Tartaros,
   In the darkest depths of the Underworld,
   I could have borne it—
   No one would have seen me or laughed at me.
   Instead I am exposed here on this mountainside,
   The winds' plaything, a source of joy

And malicious laughter to my enemies.

CHORUS:

What enemies, Prometheus? Which of the gods
Will harden his heart to laugh at you?
None but Zeus. His mind is a tyrant's;
His rule is stiff-necked, inflexible.
Until he chooses, or someone usurps his throne,
Your misery can never end.

PROMETHEUS:

It must end! One day Zeus will need me;
One day he will need to know the secret
I carry, the secret that could destroy him.
And when that day comes, he can crawl to me,
Honey my ears with soft persuasion,
And threaten me faint with fear,
But I will not give way. *He* must yield to *me*,
Call me his friend, and loose my chains himself.

CHORUS:

These are brave words, but they chill my heart.
Why should Zeus listen to reason?
He has cast you adrift in a sea of pain;
There are no harbour-lights glowing in the distance,
No beacons in sight to end your misery.

PROMETHEUS:

I know that Zeus is hard,
And believes that justice is his alone.
But one day he will yield—one day
He will run to me, confiding as a child,
As eager to offer me his friendship
As I am to be free.

CHORUS:

But what caused his anger?
What crime earned you this punishment?

Tell us, if you can bear to speak of it.

PROMETHEUS:

I can bear it: speech is no worse than silence.
When civil war began in Olympos,
And Kronos was forced to defend his throne
Against his own son, Zeus,
The Titans supported him, and came to me
For help. I tried to advise them:
My mother Themis had long foretold
That force of arms was useless—diplomacy
Was the surest way to win.
So I advised them; but they ignored me,
Preferring naked force to argument.
I joined with Zeus against them: by my plan
Tartaros opened his black jaws, and swallowed
Kronos and all his tribe. Zeus was made king
With my help—and this is how he repaid me!
All tyrants are eaten with the same disease:
They dare not trust their friends.
His father's throne was hardly warm under him
When he began rewarding his followers,
Granting each god new powers, new privileges.
Only man was forgotten—
Zeus hated him, and wanted him destroyed.
I was the only one who opposed it:
I saved mankind from the gaping jaws of hell;
I showed them mercy, and I have been shown none.

CHORUS:

Prometheus, we would need to be made of stone
To ignore your torments. You have suffered
Injustices that fill our hearts with grief.

PROMETHEUS:

I am a pitiful sight for my friends to see.

71

CHORUS:

You befriended man—was that your only crime?

PROMETHEUS:

No: I taught them to enjoy the present.
Until then they'd burrowed endlessly, like moles,
Into the secrets of a dark destiny.

CHORUS:

A strange disease—how did you cure it?

PROMETHEUS:

I gave them two priceless gifts: hope, and fire.

CHORUS:

Fire? Men have fire?

PROMETHEUS:

Fire, that will bring them knowledge.

CHORUS:

And it was for giving these gifts that Zeus—

PROMETHEUS:

Torments me, and will never set me free.

CHORUS:

Never? No end is fixed for your suffering?

PROMETHEUS:

None, unless he chooses.

CHORUS:

Unless he chooses—
How can you hope for that? You disobeyed him,
And he has the right to punish you.
All we can do is share your grief,
And look for the quickest way to end it.

PROMETHEUS:

Your advice costs you nothing: you are free.
It was I who sinned; my neck is in the noose.
When I helped mankind, I foresaw that Zeus
Would punish me—but how could I foresee

This punishment: pinned down on a giddy rock,
Alone, to watch my own life wither?
Your tears cannot help me; come down, closer,
And I will tell you the rest of my punishment.
Come down, I beg you—do not hesitate;
For Misery is a restless wanderer,
And she has settled, for a time, on me.

CHORUS:
We will come down, Prometheus.
Look: we are stepping lightly from our chariot,
Leaving the sacred pathways of the sky—
We have come down, and we will hear you.

They are now standing on firm ground at
PROMETHEUS' *feet. All at once the sound of*
approaching wings is heard.

PROMETHEUS:
Shhh! Someone else is here . . .

OKEANOS *comes in, on a winged horse.*

OKEANOS:
Prometheus, I have travelled fast and far
To see you. My horse needed no bit, no bridle;
My will was enough to guide him,
Driven on by a kinsman's sympathy
And the closer ties of warm friendship.
We need no flattery, you and I:
Tell me what help you want, and I will give it.

PROMETHEUS:
Okeanos! Have you, too, risked your life
To visit me, here in this iron land?
Look, then! Once I was called the friend of Zeus;
I helped him win his throne; I made him king—
And this is how he has rewarded me!

OKEANOS:

My advice is this, Prometheus:
You are far-seeing, and your mind is cunning—
Adapt, then! Learn to accept what has happened.
The old world has disappeared—a new king
Rules in Olympos. Barbed and bitter words
Will not help you—Zeus may be far away,
Set on his high throne many miles from here,
But he will hear you, and will answer you
With punishments that will make your sufferings now
Seem like a summer dream. Control your rage,
And look for a way to end your misery.
It is an old saying, but still a true one:
Proud speaking always earns a proud reply.
You are proud, Prometheus—and it is your pride
That has brought you down. Take my advice—
Give way. Zeus is a king, and will never yield.
Let me go to him now, and try once more
To persuade him—and while I am gone
Say nothing: you must see that foolish words
Are the surest way to earn more punishment.

PROMETHEUS:

I envy you: you are free, and blameless.
But your love for me may earn a grim reward:
Almighty Zeus is not to be persuaded—
That road is dangerous, and could destroy you.

OKEANOS:

You have always put others before yourself:
These chains prove that. But it is stubbornness
To stop your friends from helping you. Let me go—
If Zeus will listen, I will persuade him.

PROMETHEUS:

Your concern is born of true friendship,

74

And I am grateful. But do not go to Zeus—
It will not help me to see you destroy yourself.
For my friends' grief is my grief too: I weep
For the sufferings of my brother Atlas,
Who bears the whole weight of Earth and Heaven
On his groaning shoulders; I weep for Typhon,
The Hundred-headed, who left his lair
In the foothills of Cilicia to challenge Zeus.
He had grim gorgon-glances to help him,
And a hundred jaws hissing defiance—
But Zeus's thunderbolt, ringed with unsleeping fire,
Blasted the boasting from him for ever.
Now he lies pinned under the roots of Mount Etna,
Cowering fearfully from the flames above,
Where Hephaistos smithies white-hot steel
Into new weapons for his master.
Typhon has been scorched into submission,
But he will not lie broken for ever—
One day, in a river of engulfing fire,
He will awake, and Sicily will die:
Her rivers, her fields, her gentle pastureland
Will be swallowed up in a furnace of destruction.
This I foresee. One day Zeus must give way,
Forget his anger, and pardon me.
Until then, Okeanos, learn to be wise:
Zeus has punished me, but I am patient too.

OKEANOS:

Prometheus, this is stubbornness, not patience.
Soft words are a certain cure for anger.

PROMETHEUS:

Certain, yes—if the time is right. If not,
They only inflame it further.

OKEANOS:

My poor friend,
Men called you far-sighted once. Can you not see
That in taking this risk we lose nothing?

PROMETHEUS:

We lose everything! Approaching Zeus
Is mindless folly, a waste of breath.

OKEANOS:

If it is folly, then let me indulge it—
Wise men often cloak themselves in folly.

PROMETHEUS:

I would be foolish, if I let you go.

OKEANOS:

What shall I do then? Go home and leave you?

PROMETHEUS:

Yes, go home, or you will be hated too.

OKEANOS:

Hated? By whom? The new king of the gods?

PROMETHEUS:

By pitying me you risk his anger.

OKEANOS:

His anger, and a punishment like yours?

PROMETHEUS:

You understand at last. Go home now, quickly.

OKEANOS:

Already my horse is brushing the sky
With eager wings. You have left me no choice;
My heart is heavy, but I will obey you.

He goes, sadly.

CHORUS:

We are weeping for you, Prometheus:
Our cheeks are wet with a bitter dew.

76

Once the old gods ruled us;
But now Zeus has broken them for ever,
And made new laws to bolster up his tyranny.

The whole world is weeping, Prometheus,
For you and your brother Titans.
Once we were glad to honour you—but now
That honour has dwindled to a fearful memory
Cowering in the shadow of what you have suffered.

All Asia is weeping for you; in Colchis
The warrior-maidens do not hide their tears;
The forgotten peoples of Scythia,
By the barren waters of Lake Maiotis,
Have put aside their misery, and pity you.

In Arabia, too, where the flower of warriors gather;
In cities perched high on the Caucasus,
Brave warriors, hedged with living steel,
Have seen your agony, and felt their hearts
Quicken with unaccustomed grief.

One other god, one only, has suffered as you have.
Your brother Atlas challenged Zeus,
And now, till the end of time, he must carry
The whole earth's weight, and the sky above it,
A burden beyond imagining.

The restless sea, the barren depths of hell,
And the quicksilver rivers that water the earth,
Have heard him, and are weeping for him
Till the echoes bubble up to answer them;
The whole world is grieving; only Zeus is deaf.

PROMETHEUS:
    I will not go down on my knees to him.

I gave him the power he boasts of, the power
He has used against me—why should I beg
For mercy? True, I helped mankind against him;
I gave them priceless gifts, ended their fear
And ignorance, and taught them knowledge.
But where was the crime in that? Until I helped them
They had eyes, but could see nothing,
Ears, but could not hear. They blundered through life
Like the blind phantoms that visit us in dreams.
Death was the only certainty they knew;
They built no houses, had no skill in carpentry,
But lived in caves, or burrowed underground
Like termites hiding in terror from the sun.
They knew nothing of the changing seasons—
Winter, spring and summer passed them by
Like a procession half glimpsed in the moonlight.
Then I helped them:
I showed them the stars' elusive movements
And gave them the gift of numbers. I taught them
Writing, the servant of memory, and revealed
The secrets of music and poetry.
They learned from me how to tame animals
And use their greater strength to help them,
How to yoke proud horses, and train them to draw
The glittering chariots that the wealthy love.
They mastered the sea, and learned to ride it
In ships with woven wings to entice the wind.
These were the gifts I gave them: good gifts
That have ended their suffering for ever—
And yet this is a gift I cannot give myself!
CHORUS:
I pity you: you are like a physician
Who has learned how to cure every disease

78

Except the one that is eating his own life.

PROMETHEUS:

Your words are apt: for until I helped mankind
The secrets of medicine were hidden from them—
When they fell sick, they died. I taught them
To mix soothing potions to ease their pain.
I showed them all the paths of prophecy:
How to find meaning in dreams and oracles,
And interpret chance meetings on a journey;
How to learn from the flight of birds—
Which ones to trust, and which foreshadowed death.
They learned to sacrifice, and read the future
In glowing entrails; they learned to understand
The delicate spectrum of the liver and heart.
I taught them to wrap thighs in fat, and burn them
For the gods' delight; what signs to look for
In the dying embers of the altar-fire.
I gave them the wealth hidden in the earth,
Mines of iron and copper, silver and gold.
Whatever skills they know, they learned from me—

CHORUS:

And you have paid the price of your teaching.
Risk no more—one day you will be set free
With power to rival Zeus himself.

PROMETHEUS:

No: I cannot escape my destiny.
I must endure all the agonies he sends me—
Even my skill is over-ruled by Necessity.

CHORUS:

And has Necessity no overlord?

PROMETHEUS:

Yes: the Fates, and the ever-watchful Furies.

CHORUS:

Do they rule Zeus as well?

PROMETHEUS:

Even Zeus,

For all his power, must bow to destiny.

CHORUS:

What is his destiny? To rule for ever?

PROMETHEUS:

Do not ask: that secret cannot be told.

CHORUS:

You know his fate, and will not reveal it?

PROMETHEUS:

I will reveal it when the time is right.
For it is this secret that will set me free.

CHORUS:

We will never oppose Zeus:
Whatever he decrees we will obey him, gladly.
Every day, beside the sacred waters of Okeanos,
We will sacrifice,
And offer up prayers to delight the gods.

For we have chosen not to fight fate;
We have chosen to live peacefully,
Enriching our souls with the joys of quietness.
You challenged Zeus,
And he has drowned you in a sea of sorrow.

How can man save you, or repay you?
His life is a waking dream, overshadowed by evening;
Beside the gods he is powerless, a beggar
Twisted by grief—
How can he alter the will of Zeus?

Once we sang you a different song: when Hesione,
Our sister whom we loved above all others,

Left our father's home to marry you, we sang you
A wedding song—
How could we know that it would end like this?

    I O *rushes in, driven mad by the gadfly she thinks is
pursuing her.*

IO:

    Where am I now? Who lives here?
    Are you a criminal? Who chained you here?
    I have wandered far and wide over the earth—
    Tell me, what place is this?
    Aah! It is here again, the gadfly,
    Attacking me! Save me, oh save me, Earth!
    O shadow of unsleeping Argos, I fear you:
    Why are you following me?
    If the earth itself was not deep enough to bury you,
    How can I escape? I am a starving beggar
    Picking my way along a barren coastline—
    Will you never let me rest?
    All day your pipes play a drowsy song,
    But when I reach out for sleep it is snatched away.
    Zeus, lord of heaven, what have I done?
    Why are you punishing me—why is my body
    Twisted and racked with endless pain?
    Send down a thunderbolt to destroy me;
    Bury me in the earth, or scatter my flesh
    For fish to tear at—but pity me!
    I have wandered till my flesh is aching,
    Half ox, half woman. O Zeus,
    If you have eyes, look down and pity me!

PROMETHEUS:

    It is Io's voice: Io daughter of Inachos,
    Whose love warmed Zeus's heart, and earned her

Hera's undying anger. Why have you come here?
We cannot help you, and we dare not pity you.

IO:

How do you know my name? Who are you?
Your words chill my heart—
Who has told you of my punishment,
Of the pitiless gadfly that is eating my life
And allowing me no rest?
Hera has sent me mad: to ease her jealousy
I must wander the world alone,
Gnawed by unending hunger, unmarried and most
  miserable.
Many men have angered the gods,
But none have been punished as I have!
You know my name—but do you also know
What I must do or say to end my misery?
For I can bear whatever the gods inflict on me
If I only know that one day it will end.

PROMETHEUS:

I will tell you—simply, as a friend should.
I am Prometheus, who gave men fire.

IO:

Unhappy Prometheus!
And it is for this that you are punished?

PROMETHEUS:

I have spoken of my troubles already.

IO:

But not to me. Will you not tell me, too?

PROMETHEUS:

If I must, I must. What do you want to hear?

IO:

Who punished you? Who pegged you here on the cliff-
  face?

PROMETHEUS:

Hephaistos, acting under Zeus's orders.

IO:

Why? What had you done?

PROMETHEUS:

I helped mankind. There is no more to be said.

IO:

Yes, there is one thing more.
I have been punished too, condemned
To a restless wandering. When will it end?
When will the gods release me?

PROMETHEUS:

Do not ask:

It is best for you not to know the future.

IO:

Tell me! I can bear it.

CHORUS:

No, Prometheus!

First she must tell us why the gods have punished her.
After that you can show her the future.

PROMETHEUS:

Speak, Io. These are Okeanos' daughters,
Your own father's sisters. Tell them—
Shared grief is easier to bear.

IO:

It is a piteous story, but I will tell you.
Once I was beautiful: in my father's house
I was happy, warmed by the affection
Of those I loved. Then the gods turned my beauty
To corruption, and plunged me in a sea of pain.
Every night my dreams were troubled—
Ghosts hovered round me, whispering: "Io,
You are beautiful—why are you wasting your youth?

Zeus is on fire for you; he is offering you
A magnificent marriage. Go to Lerne,
Where your father's flocks browse in soft green meadows;
He will come to you there, and marry you."
Every night this dream pounded in my brain
Until, in desperation, I told my father,
And he sent messengers to Delphi and Dodona
To consult the gods. But all they brought back
Was a tangle of oracles and prophecies,
Impossible to unravel. Then at last,
Like a piercing ray of light, Apollo spoke
Clearly and simply: I was to be sent away,
Condemned to wander the world for ever,
Banished from everything I loved. If not,
A thunderbolt would come down and destroy us all.
What could my father answer? The god had spoken
And left him no choice. He called me to him,
Tears starting in his eyes, and banished me.
My appearance was changed, and my wits destroyed.
The gods gave me these horns, and sent me
This gadfly, that will never let me rest.
Since then I have wandered the world, alone,
Tormented by fate and the gods' blind frenzy.
O Prometheus,
If you know what else I must suffer,
I beg you, tell me now. Do not pity me,
Or say what you think will please me—
False words are the bitterest punishment of all.
CHORUS:
Enough, enough!
You have stabbed our hearts with pity—
How can the Fates look down on you
And know they have caused such suffering?

PROMETHEUS:
You are afraid for Io; but you are weeping too soon.
Hold back your tears until you hear the rest.

CHORUS:
Is there more? What else must she suffer?
Is there no comfort for her sickness
But the pain of knowing how it will end?

PROMETHEUS:
There is no other comfort. I must tell her
All the sufferings the gods will send her.
Listen to me, Io: you have told us the start
Of your wanderings, and now you must hear their end.
First you must travel to the rising sun,
Across the barren plains of Scythia
Where the Nomads live. They are huntsmen,
Restless wanderers who carry all they own
In wicker houses built on ox-carts.
Avoid them: your path lies further on—
Where the sea booms along the echoing shore
You will visit the savage Chalybes
And see the secret underground smithies
Where they work soft iron into a thousand shapes.
Not far from them is the River Hubris—
You must find its source, high in the Caucasus,
Where gaunt cliffs challenge the stars themselves.
On the other side the Amazons will help you;
They are warrior-women, and despise men,
And their city is eyried above Salmydessa
Where all ships die. They will give you guides,
And take you as far as Kimmeria
And the narrow entrance of Lake Maiotis.
Here, where the angry sea foams against the rocks,
You must cross the Isthmus, in a crossing

Men will remember for ever; they will call it
Bosphorus, the Crossing-place of the Ox-maiden.
This is the start of your wandering, Io:
For Zeus loves you, and he has cursed you—
When a god loves a mortal, the mortal dies.

IO:

Alas! How can I bear it?

PROMETHEUS:

There is worse to come, trouble that will tear you
In two. You are sailing on a lake of tears:
I have no comfort to offer you.

IO:

Why must I go on living? I could climb
To the top of the cliff, hurl myself down
On the resisting earth, and end my misery.
It would be a cruel death—but no more cruel
Than the living death the gods have sent me.

PROMETHEUS:

I envy you: you have dreams of death
To comfort you. But I am immortal:
I must endure all the punishments the gods
Inflict on me, so long as Zeus is king.

IO:

So long as Zeus is king? Will his power end?

PROMETHEUS:

Would that please you?

IO:

He is torturing me—how can I love him?

PROMETHEUS:

Listen, then: one day he will lose his throne.
He will marry, and his marriage will destroy him.

IO:

What marriage? To a god, or a mortal?

PROMETHEUS:

That is a question I dare not answer.

IO:

But how will his marriage destroy him?

PROMETHEUS:

He will have a son, greater than his father.

IO:

And is there no way for him to save himself?

PROMETHEUS:

Nothing but my release will save him.

IO:

Your release? But he has forbidden it.

PROMETHEUS:

One of your descendants will set me free,
Thirteen generations from now.

IO:

                                      Prometheus,
You are speaking in unguessable riddles.

PROMETHEUS:

Yes—it would hurt you to know the answers.

IO:

How can you offer me hope like this,
And then snatch it away?

PROMETHEUS:

                             No, I have said
Too much already. Do not ask for more.

CHORUS:

Why are you so reluctant to speak?
She is asking for nothing unreasonable.
Tell her the rest—no harm can come of it.

PROMETHEUS:

Very well, since you leave me no choice.
Listen, Io: the gadfly will goad you

Across the channel that links the continents,
To the eastern sea where the sun is born,
And the plains of Kisthene. You will see
Strange monsters: Phorcys' unholy daughters,
Swan-women as old as the stars, who are hated
By all who look on them. Not far away
Their gorgon-sisters live, winged and venomous;
Snakes live in their writhing locks, and all
Who see them are turned to stone. Cover your eyes
And hurry past, where fiercer beasts are waiting:
Wolf-vultures, the favourites in Zeus's menagerie,
And their prey, the one-eyed Arimaspians
Who ride swift horses beside the River of Gold.
You must not visit them; go further east
To the source of the glittering sun itself—
The river Aithiops, and the dark race
Who lived beside it, poised on the edge of the world.
Follow it as far as the mountains of Biblos,
Where the Nile, sweetest of rivers, is born.
From there you must go down into Egypt
And settle in the Land of the Two Rivers,
Where your children will live till the end of time.

Do you still say I am speaking in riddles?
If so, ask and I will explain clearly.
There is time enough—my punishment
Has given me all eternity to grieve in.

CHORUS:

If there is more to bear,
Another chapter of gnawing misery,
Tell her. She must hear everything.

PROMETHEUS:

I can outline her wanderings, and show her

The bare skeleton of what she must suffer.
But she must flesh the bones herself, and fill in
The teeming details of her own agony.
When you crossed the Molossian plains, Io,
You came to Dodona. There, on the steep sides
Of the mountain, shaggy with secret oaks,
The oracle spoke to you clearly and simply:
"Have you come, Io? One day you will be
Called holy, and honoured as the Consort of Zeus."
But even this oracle could not comfort you—
Hera sent down her gadfly, and goaded you
Along the shores of the Adriatic
To this desolate spot, driving you on
In a ceaseless winter of suffering.
Men will call that sea the Ionian,
And it will honour your name for ever.
You will settle in Egypt, where the Nile
Spreads out its arms to the welcoming sea.
Zeus will visit you there, in Canopus,
And end your misery. With a gentle hand
He will free you from madness; and at his touch
You will conceive, and bear a son,
Apis the Bull-king, who will rule
Wherever the Nile waters the fruitful earth.
His descendant Danaos, in the fifth generation—
A great king, with fifty daughters—will be forced
To flee from Egypt, and come to Argos,
To prevent his daughters' unholy marriage
With their own cousins. Blinded with lust,
And hot as eagles swooping on their prey,
The bridegrooms will pursue his daughters.
But the gods will cheat them: in Argos
Their own brides will murder them, one by one,

Cutting their throats on the wedding-night.
Only one of them will not be sacrificed:
His bride will look down on him as he sleeps,
And a warm tide of love and pity
Will check her hand. From this maiden, who chose
To be called coward instead of murderess,
A race of kings will be born to rule in Argos.
She will bear a son, Herakles the Archer,
Who will come to Scythia and set me free.

That is all I can tell you, Io:
These prophecies were taught me by Themis,
My own mother, who has seen and known
All that has happened since the world began.

I O breaks in with a wild cry of madness.

IO:

Aah! On, on! Onward!
Madness is seething in my brain again,
Twisting and writhing in the agony
Brought by the gadfly!
My heart is fluttering with a wild fear;
My eyes roll white; my tongue is loosened,
And utters a storm of words that beat
And dash themselves blindly on the rocks of Fate!
They are driving me on—I dare not linger!

She rushes out. There is a moment of silence.

CHORUS:

It was a wise man, wise beyond all others,
Who first framed this simple law:
Never try to marry above yourself—
No honest workman has ever bettered himself

By marrying a rich man's daughter.

We will never long to share Zeus's bed,
Or hope for any of the gods as husbands.
Io's fate has taught us that—
Zeus saw her, and lusted for her,
Till Hera's savage jealousy struck her down.

When we marry, it will be with our equals—
That way is safe. But the gods' love
Is like a consuming fire, a trap
From which there is no escape,
A grim battle, lost before it is fought.

PROMETHEUS:
Zeus is stiff-necked and obstinate, but still
He must yield. His marriage will break him
And topple him from his throne for ever.
As his father Kronos went into exile
He cursed his son—and that curse lives on,
And will soon be carried out. Only I
Can tell him how to escape destruction.
Till then I will let him rule, let him hug
His thunderbolts for security. Soon
Not even they will save him, or support him
As he crashes headlong into oblivion.
For he will have a terrible adversary,
Whose fire will outshine even his lightning,
And roar louder than all his thunderbolts.
The sea and the land will be shaken,
And Poseidon's trident shatter in his hand.
Zeus will stumble and fall; for he must learn
The difference between ruling and being ruled.

CHORUS:
You have no hope, and comfort yourself

91

With empty threats.

PROMETHEUS:

                        They are my only comfort—
And I will live to see them carried out.

CHORUS:

A king will arise, greater than Zeus?

PROMETHEUS:

A king who will crush him, and punish him
With torments worse than he has given me.

CHORUS:

These are bold words—are you not afraid?

PROMETHEUS:

Afraid of what? He cannot kill me.

CHORUS:

There are worse punishments he can send you.

PROMETHEUS:

Let him do his worst! I am not afraid.

CHORUS:

A wise man gives way, and bows to Necessity.

PROMETHEUS:

You be wise, then! Bow and kiss the dust
At Zeus's feet! He is less than that dust
To me. He has a little moment of ruling left—
Let him enjoy it! His end is not far away.

HERMES *comes in.*

Ah! Here comes his messenger, his flatterer,
As quick as ever to run his new master's errands.
What fearful new commands are you bringing me?

HERMES:

Prometheus, wily spinner of empty words,
Who went too far, and destroyed himself
By putting men on a pedestal above the gods;

92

Prometheus, Fire-thief, I have orders from Zeus.
You have boasted of a marriage that will destroy him,
Some miracle that will topple his throne.
You are to tell him everything, clearly,
In simple words unencumbered by riddles.

He pauses, but PROMETHEUS *says nothing.*

You would be best to speak, Prometheus—
If I go back empty-handed, you will be punished.
PROMETHEUS:
A bold speech! High-sounding rhetoric
Befitting the lackey of the gods!
Your power is newly-won, and you think it
Invincible—but so did Kronos his.
I have seen two kings hurled to destruction,
And soon I shall see a third. Run to Zeus
And tell him I despise him and all his threats—
That is the only reply I will give him.
HERMES:
We have heard insolence like this before—
You challenged Zeus, and he punished you for it.
PROMETHEUS:
I would not change my misery for yours.
Can there be anything more shameful
Than living always in another's shadow?
HERMES:
Your life is shadowed too—by this rock.
How is that better than serving Zeus?
PROMETHEUS:
Anyone can see you are his servant—
Arrogance is always courted by arrogance.
HERMES:
And are you not arrogant—proud of your agony?

93

PROMETHEUS:

Yes, I am proud of it—so proud that I hope
One day to share it with all my enemies.

HERMES:

Speak more plainly. Are you threatening me?

PROMETHEUS:

You and all the other gods I hate,
The gods who have repaid me with misery
For helping them.

HERMES:

You are insane, Prometheus—

PROMETHEUS:

Yes, if it is insane to hate my enemies.

HERMES:

Misfortune has not curbed your arrogance;
If you were free, it would outsoar the stars.

PROMETHEUS *with a cry of pain*:

Aaah!

HERMES:

Zeus is deaf to the cries of criminals.

PROMETHEUS:

The passing of time will unstop his ears;
One day he will beg to listen to me.

HERMES:

Why should he? Time has not made *you* wise.

PROMETHEUS:

No, or I would deal with the master, not the slave.

HERMES:

You will tell Zeus nothing?

PROMETHEUS *sarcastically*:

Nothing—in spite
Of all the kindnesses he has heaped on me.

HERMES:

Why are you treating me like a child?

PROMETHEUS:

It is you who are reasoning like a child,
If you expect me to speak. Nothing
Zeus can do will frighten me: I will not speak
Until he sets me free with his own hands.
He can hurl down thunderbolts to crush me,
Lash the cowering sky with lightning,
Choke the earth with snow, or destroy it
In a seething mass of overwhelming fire,
And I will endure it. Until I choose
He will never know his destroyer's name.

HERMES:

Think, Prometheus! What can you gain by this?

PROMETHEUS:

I have been given all eternity to think,
And I have made up my mind.

HERMES:

There is still time
To change it. Remember how he will punish you.

PROMETHEUS:

Save your advice for others; I am deaf.
How can you imagine I will change my mind,
Crawl to Zeus, and beg him to forgive me,
Like a woman wheedling a favour? No!
I will not do it.

HERMES:

Very well. I will waste
No more words on you. I have treated you
Leniently, and given you every chance.
But you are like a frightened horse
With the bit in its teeth, tugging the reins

95

In a desperate, hopeless longing for freedom.
Your own words have destroyed you:
All I can do now is tell you your fate—
The fate you have chosen yourself, calling
The anger of Zeus down on your own head.
He will send a thunderbolt to scorch you,
And shatter this mountainside.
You will be buried in tons of rubble, and lie
Imprisoned in darkness for a thousand years.
And when at last you see daylight again,
Still fastened to this rock, Zeus will send
An eagle to tear your flesh to rags
And feast on your liver. This punishment
Will not end until you find another god
Willing for your sake to journey into hell
And take your sufferings upon himself.
That is your reward for disobedience.
It is no idle threat; when Zeus speaks,
Whatever he ordains is carried out.
Look around you, Prometheus, and consider
Whether you still think it wise to challenge him.

CHORUS:

His advice is good: give up your anger
And learn to obey. That way is best.

PROMETHEUS:

Do you really think he has frightened me?
I was expecting this—no man
Can hope for favours from his enemies.
Zeus! where is your lightning?
Let it be hurled down on me
Like a twisted curl on the forehead of Death!
Send a thunderbolt to split the sky
And make it the winds' playground;

Open the earth, and from its roots
Awaken sleeping fire, till the sea
Boils up and drowns the stars!
I have made my choice—
Throw me into the lowest depths of hell
And chain me in darkness for ever;
For whatever you do to me
You cannot kill me!

HERMES:

He is insane: we cannot help him.
His own words have already destroyed him.

The first rumblings of the thunderstorm are heard in the distance, and he says more urgently to the CHORUS:

Daughters of Okeanos, you have shown him sympathy,
And comforted his misery;
But there is nothing more you can do for him.
Come away with me now, and leave him:
If you stay, you too will be caught
In the comet-tail of the thunderbolt.

CHORUS:

No! We will not leave him, for all your threats.
That would be a crime past bearing.
Whatever he suffers, we will suffer with him.
For he has taught us one thing—
There is nothing more abhorrent
Than turning against the friends who helped you.

HERMES:

Very well: you have made your choice.
It will be no use blaming fate
Later, when it has struck you down,
Or saying that Zeus has punished you unjustly.

You know what is going to happen,
And you have chosen destruction—
Your own foolishness has destroyed you;
I can do no more!

As he goes, the thunder moves overhead, and jagged flashes of lightning bathe PROMETHEUS *and the* CHORUS *in eerie silhouette.*

PROMETHEUS:
Look! What he prophesied is happening:
The earth is writhing and groaning
Like a man in torment,
Throwing up tortured echoes
From deep in its heart.
The fires of lightning are flickering all round us;
Whirlwinds are hugging columns of dust
In a dervish-dance of destruction,
As the thunderbolt shatters the sky
And drinks up the swollen sea.
O Themis my mother; O sun and moon
Who give light and life to all men—
Look down on me now:
Look down on the injustice I am suffering!

In a final tremor the earth splits apart, and PROMETHEUS' *rock vanishes in a cloud of dust and rubble. When the air clears and there is silence, the stage is deserted.*

MEDEA

NOTE

In the year of *Medea*'s first production, 431 B.C., the Peloponnesian War began. By then, as a result of fifty years of unbroken prosperity, the Athenians had come to regard themselves as the greatest, most favoured people in Greece—an attitude which is reflected in Jason's words to Medea on p. 118. Although he is talking of Corinth, the view he expresses was that held by most of Euripides' audience about their own role in the world.

Euripides was famous for his insight into the female mind, and the careful psychological motivation of his characters. In this play the contrast with Sophocles and Aeschylus is especially noticeable: Medea is moved to vengeance by human feelings arising from her own character and situation; she is not, like Prometheus and Oedipus, a helpless victim of the gods' anger.

There are other differences too. The Chorus, for example, play a much less significant role. Their comments on the action are more perfunctory, less integrated with the main scenes of the play. This stylisation even leads to a most unlikely dramatic situation: no real group of Corinthian women, seeing their king threatened by a barbarian stranger, would have kept quiet and sympathised with the outsider. Clearly for Euripides the Chorus provided no more than decoration and relaxation after the dramatic tension of the main scenes.

And the main scenes *are* dramatic. The confrontations of Medea and Jason (p. 117, p. 142), and the subtle touches of character in small parts like Aigeus and the Tutor, show Euripides' ability at its highest. Medea's soliloquies, too

101

(p. 110, p. 133), are very fine, and were widely imitated by later authors.

Another important innovation was the prologue, where—as Aristophanes makes Euripides say in *The Frogs*—"the first person on stage told the audience exactly what to expect". The prologue to this play is a good example: the old Nurse comes distractedly out of the palace, and in a long monologue sets the scene for the watching audience . . .

MEDEA

Characters in order of appearance:

NURSE
TUTOR
MERMEROS ⎫ *Medea's children*
PHERES ⎭
MEDEA, *a princess of Colchis*
CREON, *king of Corinth*
JASON, *Medea's husband*
AIGEUS, *king of Athens*
SERVANT *of king Creon*
CHORUS *of Corinthian women*
Guards

MEDEA

A courtyard of Medea's palace in Corinth. At one side of the stage is an altar to Earth and Sky, the gods whose worship she brought with her from Colchis. As the play begins, her old NURSE *comes out to pray at this altar.*

NURSE:

If only the Argo had never sailed,
Never winged her way past the Clashing Rocks
To Colchis; if only the pine-trees
Had been left undisturbed on Mount Pelion,
And not been cut down to build her!
No expedition would have been sent to fetch
The golden fleece; Jason and Medea
Would never have fallen in love, or gone
To Iolkos. She would never have persuaded
Pelias' daughters to kill their own father,
Never had to flee here to Corinth
With Jason and her children, to escape
Death, and honour the man she married.

But not even Medea could escape her fate:
Everything she loves has turned against her.
Jason has rejected her and the children,
Infatuated with love for Glauke,
The daughter of Creon who rules this land.
Poor lady! She has been abandoned, left
To mourn for the marriage-vows he made her,
The promises he broke. She will eat nothing;
She weeps the days away, dragging herself
From room to room like a wounded animal.
She dresses in rags, and keeps her eyes

Fixed endlessly on the ground, as deaf
To the advice of those who love her
As a stone, or the barren sea itself.
She talks of nothing but her native land,
And the home and father she betrayed
When she married Jason, who has rejected her.
Now, too late, her misery has taught her
That she should never have sailed from Colchis.
She hates the children, and will not see them;
She is a princess, not used to misery,
And I am afraid of the revenge she is planning—
Suicide perhaps, in some dark corner,
Or the double murder of Jason and Glauke.
Whatever it is, they should fear her:
She had enemies before, and they are dead.

Ah! Here come the children now. They have been
Playing, untouched by their mother's distress—
They are too young to understand such misery.

    Medea's two sons M E R M E R O S *and* P H E R E S *come in
with their* T U T O R.

TUTOR:
  Nurse, you are Medea's most trusted servant—
  Why are you wandering out here alone?
  Has she sent you away? Will she not allow
  Even you to be with her and share her grief?
NURSE:
  You are a wise man, wise enough for Jason
  To have chosen you as his children's tutor.
  Can you not understand that a good slave
  Is always grieved to see his masters suffer?
  I could not bear it: I came out here

To tell her sufferings to the gods above.

TUTOR:

She is suffering now—but what will she do
When she hears what else the gods have sent her?

NURSE:

Is there something else? Tell me, I beg you.

TUTOR:

No, no. She has enough to bear already.

NURSE:

I will keep it secret, if I have to.

TUTOR:

I was walking by the Fountain of Peirene,
Where the old men sit and throw dice in the sun,
When I overheard them talking. They were saying—
And it may be no more than idle talk—
That Creon is planning to banish Medea
And her children from Corinth for ever.

NURSE:

But Jason will never let him harm the children!
He hates Medea—does he hate them too?

TUTOR:

He has forgotten how he used to love them:
They are her children, and that is enough.

NURSE:

How can I tell Medea this news?

TUTOR:

There is no need. She will hear soon enough.

NURSE:

Poor lambs! Why does your father hate you?
He is my master, and I must honour him—
But can he not see how unjust this is?

TUTOR:

Surely you know that all men are the same,

Interested in nothing but themselves?
Jason has Glauke—he has forgotten the children.

The CHILDREN *begin to cry, and the* NURSE *takes them in her arms.*

NURSE:
There, there, my darlings. Go inside now—
Everything will be all right. (To the TUTOR) Take them in,
But keep them away from their mother.
There is a wild look in her eyes, as though
She is planning some terrible revenge.
She is angry, and someone will suffer for it—
Pray god it is her enemies, not those she loves!

MEDEA *from inside:*
O Zeus! Can you see my suffering?
Can you see the grief that is eating my life?

NURSE:
My little ones, your poor mother
Is distracted with grief.
Go in—but keep away from her.
If she sees you, her anger
May make her harm even you.
She had enough to bear before;
But this new grief will crush her
And fill her heart with misery.
Go inside now, quickly.

The TUTOR *takes the* CHILDREN *into the palace.*

MEDEA *from inside:*
O Justice, who lives with the gods above,
I am lost, embarked without hope

On a stormy sea of suffering.
The children must die—
Their father has betrayed me, and he
And all his house must be destroyed.

NURSE:

My lady, this is unjust. How have
The children shared their father's guilt?
Why do you hate them? O my little ones,
I am afraid for you. Your mother
Is used to ruling, not being ruled,
And this sorrow has stabbed her heart.
Kings and queens live with great events,
And their character is shaped by them.
But I am happy to be poor:
I will grow old untouched
By the hand of Fate.
Moderation is Man's greatest gift;
Pride will bring him no profit—
It will only anger the gods
And destroy him and all his house.

The CHORUS *come in.*

CHORUS:

We heard Medea's voice
In a desperate cry of pain
From inside the palace.
What has happened, Nurse?
What has caused her grief?
We love her, and her suffering
Has filled our hearts with pity.

NURSE:

She has lost everything:
Jason has taken a mistress

108

And left her to weep her life away.
She will not be comforted,
Even by those who love her most.

MEDEA *from inside*:
Zeus, lord of heaven,
Why do you not kill me now?
Send a thunderbolt to destroy me—
I am surrounded by misery,
And death is my only comfort.

CHORUS:
This is a terrible prayer:
Death comes soon enough to men
And needs no prayers to hasten it.

MEDEA *from inside*:
The husband I loved and honoured,
Who swore to love me for ever,
Has betrayed me, and must be punished.
He must die beside his mistress,
Crushed by the ruins of their own palace.

NURSE:
These are terrible words:
She is full of wild anger,
And it can only lead to death.

CHORUS:
Go in, Nurse: ask her to come out
And speak with us. Go quickly,
Before the doom she is threatening
Comes down and engulfs us all.

NURSE:
She is angry, and will not listen
Even to her own faithful servants.
But I will do as you ask,
And try to persuade her to speak with you.

She goes in.

CHORUS:
> Medea's grief is terrible,
> A lonely, echoing lament
> Against the husband who betrayed her.
> But she will be revenged:
> She has invoked Justice,
> The unsleeping consort of Zeus,
> And the gods will answer her prayer.

> MEDEA *comes out of the palace.*

MEDEA:
> Women of Corinth, you asked me to come out
> And I have obeyed you. For I would not
> Have you think I am proud—that reputation
> Is too easily earned. Some men live quietly
> At home, keeping themselves to themselves,
> And their neighbours call them standoffish.
> Others, who live in the public eye,
> Do more harm to their own reputations
> With a single haughty look, than with all
> Their years of devoted service to the state.
> I am a stranger here, and must follow
> Your customs: for all men distrust strangers.
> My life has been tainted with disaster—
> I lived for the love in Jason's eyes,
> And he has deserted me, leaving me
> Nothing but death to cling to.

> Of all the living beings in the world,
> Women are surely the most unhappy.
> We are so afraid of dying old maids

That we struggle to save ourselves a dowry,
And then use it to buy ourselves into slavery.
Pure chance decides whether our husbands
Turn out good or bad—and once
We have married them, they are ours for life.
Marriage is like a strange new country,
With none of the familiar landmarks of home
To guide us through it. We must learn
To live in peace with our husbands,
Or we make our own lives a martyrdom.
A man can escape from a nagging wife
By going out and relaxing with his friends;
But a woman lives in her husband's shadow,
And depends on him alone for happiness.
They say that our reward for this
Is a quiet life, and that we leave
Pain and suffering to men—but I say
It is better to fight a thousand enemies
Than bear a single child.

It is different for you: this is your city,
And your homes and friends are here
To surround you with a cocoon of love.
But I have no city: I am an alien,
A stranger whose husband has deserted her.
I have no family or friends to turn to:
All I can do is ask you one favour—
If I can find some way to punish Jason
For what he did to me, keep it secret.
They say that women are weak and timid,
Afraid of violence; but when our marriage
Crumbles in ruins, we find new strength,
And our enemies are right to fear us.

CHORUS:
>We will do as you ask, Medea—
>The revenge you are planning is a just one.
>But here comes King Creon, to bring you more grief.

CREON *comes out of the palace, with his attendants.*

CREON:
>They told me you were out here, Medea,
>Thinking poisonous thoughts, and furious
>With Jason. I have come to tell you this:
>You are to take your children and leave Corinth
>For ever—I will not go home again
>Until you have crossed our borders into exile.

MEDEA:
>O Zeus! Is there nowhere for me to turn?
>My enemies are closing in; the noose
>Is tightening—is there no escape?
>You hate me, Creon. But answer me this:
>What have I done? Why are you banishing me?

CREON:
>Bluntly, I am afraid of you, afraid
>Of the harm you may do my daughter.
>And it is no idle fear: you are subtle,
>Trained in witchcraft, and driven to despair
>By the way your husband has treated you.
>I know what you are planning: my spies have told me
>How you have sworn to be revenged on us all,
>Bride, father and bridegroom. You are a threat,
>Medea—a threat that must be removed
>Before it is too late. Those are my reasons.

MEDEA:
>Is that all? You are afraid of me?

Creon, I have lived with people's hatred
All my life. I have many strange skills,
And I have always been mistrusted by those
Who do not understand them. But not you,
Creon! What need have you to fear me?
No one but a fool would attack a king.
Besides, I have no quarrel with you—
You gave your daughter to the man I hate,
But it was Jason who betrayed me, not you.
I pray to almighty Zeus that this marriage
May bring good luck to the three of you—
And in return I ask you humbly for one favour:
If I keep quiet, forget the wrongs
I have suffered, and bow to your authority,
Let me stay in Corinth—do not banish me!

CREON:
Your words are mild, but I am still afraid
Of the anger buried deep in your heart.
I trust you even less than before, Medea:
Your anger can be dealt with, but your smiles
Are dangerous. There is no more to say:
You are my enemy, and must leave Corinth—
Not even your "strange skills" will prevent it.

MEDEA:
Please let me stay—for Glauke's sake!

CREON:
You are wasting your breath. I will not give way.

MEDEA:
You will not listen? You will banish me?

CREON:
Yes: I must put my own family first.

MEDEA:
O Colchis! Why did I ever leave you?

CREON:

You love your native land, and I love mine.

MEDEA:

Love is the bitterest gift a man can have.

CREON:

That depends on what the Fates decide.

MEDEA:

They know who is the guilty one, this time.

CREON:

Be careful: I am beginning to lose my temper.

MEDEA:

Your temper! As if that was all that mattered!

CREON:

Slaves, take her away! There is no more to say.

MEDEA:

No, Creon, no! I beg you, on my knees . . .

CREON:

You are only making things worse for yourself.

MEDEA:

I will leave Corinth—but please listen to me!

CREON:

Listen to you? How can that help you?

MEDEA:

Let me stay in Corinth for one more day,
To think about my exile, and make plans
For the children's welfare. Their father
Has disowned them, no longer interested
In whether they live or die. Pity them:
You are a father too. You have banished me,
And I accept your decision. All I ask
Is time to make plans for the children's future.

CREON:

Sometimes it is hard to know what is best.

I have shown mercy before, and regretted it.
But I will do as you ask, and endure
The consequences. Listen to me, Medea:
You can stay in Corinth for one more day,
But if by dawn tomorrow you and the children
Have not left the city, you will die.
I am afraid of you—but in a single day
You will not have time enough to harm me.

He goes inside.

CHORUS:
Unhappy Medea, we pity you.
Where will you go?
Whom can you turn to now?
Where will you find a new land to settle in,
A new people to welcome you?
In your arid desert of troubles
Where will you find an oasis of comfort?

MEDEA:
I am trapped, surrounded by disaster
On every side. There is only one gleam
Of hope: Jason and his bride are doomed,
And all who love them will die with them.
Do you think I would have gone on my knees
And crawled to Creon, except for my own ends?
He could have banished me today, and blocked
My plans; but now I have all the time I need
To send the three of them down to hell,
The newly-married bride, her father,
And my false husband who dotes on her.

There are so many ways I can kill them:
I can burn the palace round them, or creep
Into the bedroom where they lie entwined

115

And let my knife drink their blood.
But no! Both these ways are dangerous:
If I am seen in the palace, I will die,
And be cheated of my revenge. Poison is best:
I have used it before, and know its secrets.

And once I have killed them, where shall I go?
Who will take me in, and protect me
Against Creon's angry followers? No, no,
I must wait a little while. If I can find
A safe place to escape to, I will poison them;
But if there is nowhere in the world to hide,
I will gather up all my courage, and use
A sword on them. For they must die, all of them—
I am Medea, daughter of the Sun;
How can they harm me, and not suffer for it?
I swear by Hecate, the dark goddess
I have known and honoured all my life,
That I will make this a bitter marriage,
Make Creon regret the day he banished me.

CHORUS:

Chaos is walking everywhere in the world;
Great rivers are turning in their beds
And flowing backwards from the sea,
Seeking their source again.
Right and wrong have changed places,
And all men's promises are worthless.

When you sailed from Colchis, Medea,
Nursing black anger in your heart,
You passed the Clashing Rocks, and came
To Corinth and betrayal.
Jason has taken Glauke into his bed,
And condemned you to endless misery.

116

Now you are alone in a strange land,
A homeless exile with no comfort;
Jason enticed you from Colchis
With promises of love, and broke them.
Truth and Justice have abandoned Greece
And fled for ever from the sight of men.

JASON *comes out of the palace.*

JASON:
Medea, will you never learn to give way?
All you had to do was obey Creon,
And he would have let you stay in Corinth,
Here in your own home. But you threatened him,
And now he has no choice but to banish you.
I tried to persuade him to let you stay,
But he refused. All I can do now
Is see that you and the children lack nothing:
Exile is bad enough without poverty.
I know you hate me, more than any man alive,
But I will not stand by and see you suffer.

MEDEA:
You coward! Is that all you have to say?
Is that what you screwed up all your courage
To come and tell me? I hate you, Jason:
I hate you for being afraid of me,
Too afraid to take the consequences
Of your own actions! Once I loved you:
When you and your companions sailed to Colchis
To yoke the fiery bulls in the field of death
And steal the golden fleece, I helped you.
I killed the dragon, and gave you the fleece;
I ran away from my father and my people
And went with you to Iolkos. There

117

I persuaded Pelias' daughters to kill
Their own father, so that you could escape.
Ever since I met you, I have put
My love for you before my own good sense—
And how have you repaid me?
I should have been the happiest woman in Greece,
Honoured by her husband, and secure
In a marriage nothing could destroy.
Have you forgotten the promises you made me,
Marriage-oaths in the name of all the gods?
You should remember them—you made them
Again, to Glauke, not so long ago.
I have brought you a wedding-present, Jason:
Your own children's exile—their misery,
And the curse of the woman you once loved!

CHORUS:

No anger is worse, or harder to bear, than that
Of two people whose love has turned to hate.

JASON:

I see I must be careful how I answer:
I must be like a wise sea-captain,
Take in sail and hug the coast, to escape
The storms of your anger. You helped me once,
And I am grateful. But consider this:
Have I not given you more than you gave me?
I brought you from a barbarian land
To Greece, the cradle of civilisation;
Here you learned justice, the rule of law,
And all the blessings of democracy.
The Greeks understand your skills, and honour you
For them—if you had stayed in Colchis
They would have remained unknown. Great riches,
Or a voice surpassing even Orpheus',

Are wasted if no one knows about them.
These are the favours I have done you—
Do you still call my marriage a crime?
I can prove to you how wise it was,
How necessary, for your and the children's sake.

MEDEA:

Jason . . .

JASON:

Let me finish. When I came here
I was surrounded by trouble and danger—
What greater security could I have found
Than marriage with the king's own daughter?
I married Glauke to protect us all,
Medea—not because I was tired of you,
Or wanted other children. I hoped this marriage
Would give us all the chance to live in peace,
Honoured and respected as the king's friends;
I hoped to give our sons a good education,
The upbringing they deserve, instead of
Dragging out their lives in miserable exile.
You are angry with me—but only because
You do not understand. Your pride is hurt,
And, like a woman, you ignore the truth
And strike out at those who love you most.

CHORUS:

These are clever words, Jason; but we still think
That you have treated Medea unjustly.

MEDEA:

Clever words? His cleverness doubles his offence.
Your eloquence is wasted on me, Jason:
I can destroy your whole case with one question.
If the reasons for this marriage were just,
Why did you keep it so secret? Why

Did you not ask if I was willing too?

JASON:

You, willing? How could you have been willing,
When even now you cannot hide your rage?

MEDEA:

Now tell us the real reason: you were afraid
Of the harm a foreign wife would do
Your reputation as you grew older.

JASON:

I tell you that had nothing to do with it.
I married Glauke for *your* protection,
And to give our children royal brothers.

MEDEA:

How can you protect me by destroying me?
Or did you really think a broken heart
Was all I needed to make me happy?

JASON:

Now you are being foolish. I helped you,
Only to have my kindness thrown in my face;
I offered you security, and you laughed at me.

MEDEA:

I, laughed at you? Is it you, or I,
That Creon has driven into exile?

JASON:

You—and you chose that fate yourself.

MEDEA:

How did I choose it? Did I betray *you*?

JASON:

You cursed the king, and must suffer for it.

MEDEA:

Yes, and my curse extends to you as well.

JASON:

This argument is pointless. I have offered

You and the children all the help I can.
You have only to ask, and I will give you
Letters to my friends overseas, asking them
To take you in and offer you a home.
Only a madwoman would refuse this offer.

MEDEA:

Madwoman or not, I spit on your friends,
Their homes, and everything else they offer me.
I will not accept favours from a criminal.

JASON:

Very well: I have offered you help, here
At the gods' altar, and you have rejected it.
They know who is to blame, who will not take
Favours when they are offered, who has chosen
Pain and misery instead of a life of ease.

MEDEA:

Go inside—I can see you are panting
With eagerness to get back to your bride!
Or have you forgotten you are a bridegroom?
If as you say the gods know who is to blame,
They will soon punish you as you deserve.

With a last despairing gesture, JASON *goes inside.*

CHORUS:

Love is the deadliest of goddesses;
Nothing can appease her anger.
When she bends her golden bow
No man can escape destruction.

When the gods hate a mortal
They curse him with the gift of passion,
And he is soon destroyed.
But to those they love they send

121

Moderation, their most precious gift,
And allow them a quiet life.

O Zeus, send us moderation!
Send us no strife, no implacable anger,
No longing for a stranger's bed.

Medea loved, and was betrayed;
Now she is suffering a living death,
Unwept, unpitied by those she loved.
We have learned from her misery
That exile from home and friends
Is a hardship too great to bear.

A man must honour his friends
And open his heart to them,
Or be hated for ever. That is
The gods' law, and it cannot be broken.

AIGEUS *comes in.*

AIGEUS:
Medea, greetings! I am glad to see you.
MEDEA:
Aigeus! What brings you here to Corinth?
AIGEUS:
I have been to Delphi, to consult the god.
MEDEA:
What did you ask him? What is troubling you?
AIGEUS:
I have been childless for many years.
MEDEA:
Childless? But you have a wife—
AIGEUS:

I have.

MEDEA:
And did Apollo help you?

AIGEUS:
He sent me
An oracle, impossible to understand.

MEDEA:
What was it? Or must you keep it secret?

AIGEUS:
I can tell you. You are a prophetess—
Perhaps you can explain it. He told me
Not to unfasten the wineskin's foot
Until I was back in my own native land.

MEDEA:
And despite that you have come here to Corinth?

AIGEUS:
An old friend lives here, Pittheus of Troezen.

MEDEA:
Yes, Pelops' son. Everyone here respects him.

AIGEUS:
I want to see him and tell him the oracle.

MEDEA:
He is an experienced prophet: if anyone
Can tell you what Apollo meant, it is he.

Suddenly her voice grows faint, and she stumbles.

AIGEUS:
Medea! What is the matter?

MEDEA:
My husband . . .

AIGEUS:
Jason? What about him?

MEDEA:
He has betrayed me;

123

He has taken a mistress, and rejected me.

AIGEUS:

But whatever made him turn against you?

MEDEA:

I don't know. All I can tell you is
That all his love for me has turned to hate.

AIGEUS:

But who is this mistress? Whom has he chosen?

MEDEA:

A king's daughter. He is in love with power.

AIGEUS:

Which king?

MEDEA:

Creon, the ruler of Corinth.

AIGEUS:

Creon! You have good reason for your grief.

MEDEA:

And there is more. I have been banished.

AIGEUS:

Who by? Who has committed such a crime?

MEDEA:

Creon—the same Creon.

AIGEUS:

But did Jason
Do nothing to stop him?

MEDEA:

He says he tried,
But I know in his heart he agrees with him.
I beg you, Aigeus, on my knees I beg you
To pity me. If my suffering moves you,
Take me in, shelter me in your own home.
I promise you this: if you help me now
I will end your childlessness. I am skilled

In the arts of witchcraft, and can give you
A potion to bring you the sons you long for.
AIGEUS:
Medea, even without this promise
I would have been eager to help you.
The gods, and the laws of friendship, demand it.
And if it means I can have children,
The one thing in all the world I long for . . .
Listen: I can do nothing for you here
In Corinth, where I am a stranger too.
But if you can escape, and make your way
To Athens, my own country, where I am king,
I will give you a home, and protect you
Against anyone who tries to take you back.
MEDEA:
Aigeus! will you swear this by the gods?
AIGEUS:
Is my word not enough? Do you not trust me?
MEDEA:
I trust you—but I am afraid of Creon,
And of the vengeance of Pelias' daughters.
My enemies are strong, and I am weak:
I will not feel safe unless you give me
Your solemn oath, here on the gods' altar,
That you will protect me if they try to harm me.
AIGEUS:
If that is what you want, I will do it.
What is the oath? I am ready.
MEDEA:
                                    Swear, then,
Here on this altar, to Earth and the Sun,
That you will never banish me yourself,
And never let my enemies take me

From your land, while you are alive to stop them.

AIGEUS:

I swear by Earth and the Sun's majesty
To do as you ask; and if I break
My oath, I pray that the gods will destroy me.

MEDEA:

Aigeus, thank you. Now I am satisfied.
I have things to attend to in Corinth;
When they are done, I will meet you in Athens.

CHORUS:

May Hermes, guide of travellers,
Take you safely home, Aigeus;
And may the gods grant you
All the happiness you long for.
For you have shown today
That you are an honest man.

AIGEUS goes.

MEDEA:

O Zeus, and Justice his consort,
O sun and moon, can you see me now?
The work is begun—it will not be long
Before all my enemies are destroyed.
Then, when I have fed my soul with vengeance,
I will escape to Aigeus in Athens.
First I will send a servant for Jason;
When he comes I will be gentle with him,
Tell him I have changed my mind, support
What he has done, and praise his marriage.
I will beg him to let the children stay
In Corinth—not because I am willing
To leave them surrounded by my enemies,
But because I must use them to kill Glauke.

126

They will take her bride-gifts—a golden crown
And a silken robe—and they will beg her
To pity them, and let them stay here.
But when she tries on the presents, she will die,
With anyone else who touches her.
For I have smeared them with deadly poison
That will eat like fire into her soft flesh
And give me the revenge I long for. Next—
And I shudder at the thought—I must kill
The children too: no one else will have them!
So Jason and all his house will die,
And I will leave Corinth, famous for ever
As the mother who murdered her own sons.
That is my revenge on Jason, my revenge
For enticing me here from Colchis.
He will never see his children alive again—
And he will beget no brothers for them,
For Glauke is to die, twisted and racked
By my poison. I will be as gentle
As a dove to my friends; but my enemies
Will find me harder than flint itself.

CHORUS:

We are your friends, Medea, and we beg you
In the name of that friendship not to do this.

MEDEA:

I must do it. If you had been treated
As I have, you would be merciless too.

CHORUS:

But surely you will not kill the children?

MEDEA:

It is the quickest way to hurt their father.

CHORUS:

And to break your own heart . . .

MEDEA:

My heart is a stone,
Shattered beyond repair by what has happened.
Nurse! Nurse!

The NURSE *hurries out of the palace.*

NURSE:

My lady?

MEDEA:

Fetch Jason out here—
And if you love me, tell him nothing else
Except that I want to see him.

NURSE:

Yes, my lady.

She goes in.

CHORUS:
Where will you go? Who will take you in?
What city or people will welcome you,
A woman who killed her own children?
Think of striking their soft bodies—
Think of the blood spurting out!
We beg you, Medea, in heaven's name,
Do not kill them.

When they stand in front of you,
Gazing up at you with trusting eyes,
Will *your* eyes not be filled with tears?
When they realise what you are planning,
And fall on their knees for mercy,
Where will you find the strength
To murder them?

JASON *comes out of the palace.*

JASON:

　　You sent for me, and I have come. I know
　　You hate me, but I will still hear you out.
　　What is it?

MEDEA:

　　　　　　　Jason, I beg you: forgive me
　　For what I said before. We loved each other once—
　　Remember that, and bear with my anger.
　　It was madness—I see that now—to think
　　I was self-sufficient, able to curse
　　The king and survive, able to refuse
　　The help my own husband offered. But now
　　I can see why you planned this marriage—
　　How it was for my own protection,
　　And to give my children royal brothers.
　　It was foolish of me to oppose it:
　　From the start I should have shared your plans,
　　Worked for their fulfilment, and then offered
　　You and your bride my humble obedience.
　　But I let anger over-rule my common sense,
　　And now I know I was wrong. Forgive me.
　　Nurse! Nurse! Bring the children out here.

　　The NURSE *does so.*

　　My little ones, come and greet your father.
　　Once he and I were enemies—but now
　　All our anger is gone. That's right, take his hand . . .
　　　(aside) O Zeus, I am so afraid! They must die—
　　All the love in the world will not save them.
　　My heart is bursting; I cannot keep back
　　My tears. *(To the* CHILDREN*)* Do you see, my darlings?
　　　Look:

My quarrel with your father is over,
And I cannot keep the tears from my eyes.
CHORUS:
Our eyes, too, are red with weeping. Pray god
There is nothing worse than this to suffer.
JASON:
Medea, I am pleased with this change of heart.
And yet I do not blame you for being angry—
All women lose their tempers easily.
But now you have realised you were wrong,
And given way—and I praise you for it.
My sons, I have been working, with the gods,
For your future. One day you and your brothers
Will be honoured as princes of Corinth—
With the gods' help, I will see you grow up
Noble and brave, to conquer all my enemies . . .
Why are you weeping, Medea? Your cheeks
Are wet with tears. Does what I say not please you?
MEDEA:
It is nothing. I was thinking of the children.
JASON:
They are in my care. You have nothing to fear.
MEDEA:
Will you help them, then? It is Creon's will
That I should be banished, and not live here
To disturb his peace of mind and your marriage.
But surely the children are innocent—
Will you not beg Creon to let them stay,
Here, where their own father can protect them?
JASON:
I will try—but why should he listen to me?
MEDEA:
If he refuses, tell your wife to plead with him.

JASON:

Will she obey me?

MEDEA:

Yes: for I will send her gifts,
The finest in the world, a silken robe
And a golden crown. The boys will take them.
Nurse, go in and fetch them.

The NURSE *goes in, and comes back with the gifts.*

The Sun himself
Gave them to my father; he gave them to me;
And now Glauke will call herself twice-blessed:
Once because you are her husband, and once
Because she owns the gifts of the Sun himself.
Here, boys, take these presents to her: I know
That she will not refuse them.

JASON:

You fool! Why are you giving them away?
Do you think Glauke has no gold of her own,
No fine robes to wear? Keep them for yourself—
If she will not listen to her own husband,
No gold in all the world will make her help you!

MEDEA:

You are wrong. Even the gods accept gifts.
Among men, a single ounce of gold is worth
A thousand arguments. My sons are worth more
To me than gold—I would give up my life
To save them, if it was needed. Now, boys,
You must go quickly into that house of wealth,
And beg your father's new wife, my mistress,
To let you stay in Corinth. Give her the gifts—
Into her own hands. Go inside now,
And hurry back to bring me the news

I long for, news that my plans have worked.

The CHILDREN *go in with* JASON *and the* NURSE.

CHORUS:
Now no hope is left for the children:
They have taken the first step
Forward into extinction.
Jason's unhappy bride will accept the gifts,
Clutch her own death to her, and bind
Destruction as an ornament in her own fair hair.

The soft folds of the robe will enchant her,
And the glitter of the gold catch her eye;
She will deck herself in bride's clothing,
And prepare for her marriage with Death.
She cannot escape:
Hell's jaws are gaping wide to swallow her.

We pity you, Jason: when you married
King Creon's daughter, you were like
A blind man on the edge of a precipice.
You knew nothing of the misery
You were bringing her, the painful death
You were causing your own sons.

And we pity you too, Medea:
Because your husband betrayed you,
Because he rejected you and married Glauke,
You have been forced to take a revenge
That will tear your own heart in two—
You have been forced to kill your own children.

The TUTOR *comes out with the* CHILDREN.

TUTOR:
My lady, your sons are not to be banished!

When they took the presents in to Glauke
She was pleased, and promised to protect them.

MEDEA:

O Zeus!

TUTOR:

What is the matter? Is this not good news?

MEDEA:

No, no!

TUTOR:

Was I wrong to tell you?

MEDEA:

No: you have done
What you had to do—you are not to blame.

TUTOR:

Medea! My lady! Why are you weeping?

MEDEA:

I am weeping for the misery to come.

TUTOR:

What misery? Your sons will look after you.

MEDEA:

I have others to look after first.

TUTOR:

You are not the only woman who has had
To leave her children. Mankind is born to grief.

MEDEA:

Perhaps. Go in now: they are waiting for you.

The TUTOR *goes in, leaving her alone with the*
CHILDREN.

O my sons, my sons, you are safe! You have
A home at last, a city to call your own.
It is your mother who must go into exile,
To drag out her life far from the sons she loves!

I will never smile at your happiness
As you grow to manhood; when you marry
It will not be your mother who prepares
Your bride and carries the wedding-torch.
O my children, why did I bear you? Why
Did I endure the savage pains of childbirth?
Was it because of the hopes I had—
That you would protect me when I was old,
And close my eyes in death, the one blessing
All men long for? Now all my hopes are dead.
Say goodbye to your mother: your lives
Are set on a different course. Alas!
Why are you smiling at me? O my friends,
What shall I do? When I look at them
My resolution falters: I cannot kill them.
Why should I hurt them just to grieve their father,
And destroy myself as well? They must live;
I will take them away with me from Corinth.
Farewell, my former plans! And yet, and yet . . .
My enemies must be punished. O Zeus,
Let me be strong! Let me finish my sacrifice
To the dark gods of hell. My sons must die—
By my own hand. There is no alternative.
Already the crown is on Glauke's head;
Already she is writhing in agony,
Tormented by the death I sent her.
I must follow this path to the end,
And send my sons on their last, long journey.
Where are you, my children? Speak to me,
Give me your hands . . . O my little ones,
My sons, how can I bear to leave you?
How can I bear never to touch your hands,
Never to stroke your cheeks, or kiss your soft lips

Again? Leave me, leave me now. Go inside.

The CHILDREN *go in.*

How will I learn to endure such misery?
I know that what I am planning is a crime,
But I have been trapped by my own anger—
The gods have crushed me; there is no escape.

CHORUS:
Happy are those who have never known
The curse of children:
They are the sweetest sorrow known to man.

For parents can never sleep easily;
Night and day their offspring fret them
And destroy their rest.

A young child, now: will he grow up
Good or bad? How well will he survive
The storms of adolescence?

And if he grows up noble and honest,
Will the gods of hell not be jealous
And take him for their own?

Surely, measured against such a sorrow,
All the joys children bring
Should be counted as nothing?

A SERVANT *rushes in from the palace.*

SERVANT:
Medea! Where is my lady Medea?
MEDEA:
Here. What is it? What is your news?
SERVANT:
Medea, you must leave Corinth at once.

You have committed a terrible crime—
Leave, before it is too late!

MEDEA:

What has happened?

SERVANT:

Glauke, and Creon her father, are dead
From the poison you gave them.

MEDEA:

Is this true?
If so, you are my friend for ever!

SERVANT:

My lady, do you know what you are saying?
You have destroyed the royal house of Corinth—
Are you not afraid?

MEDEA:

Tell me how they died,
Every detail. When the children came in . . .

SERVANT:

When the children came in with their father
They went straight to Glauke's royal apartments.
We servants were delighted: the rumour
Buzzed round the palace that you and Jason
Had ended your quarrel, and everything
Was all right again. We followed the children,
Kissing their hands and stroking their hair
In our joy. They hurried to see Glauke.
At first she did not notice them: she had eyes
Only for Jason. When he showed her them,
Her eyes blazed with anger, and she turned away.
Jason tried to soothe her. "Glauke, my dearest,"
He said, "don't be cruel to those who love you.
Be kind to them—for my sake. Take their gifts,
And beg Creon your father not to banish them."

Glauke turned round. When she saw the presents
Her anger evaporated, and she smiled
At Jason, and promised to do as he asked.
Father and children left, and at once
She took the embroidered robe and put it on,
And set the royal crown on her head.
She called for a mirror, and arranged her hair
Under the crown, smiling at the dead image
She saw in the polished bronze. She stood up,
And began skipping up and down the room,
Stopping every now and then to admire the dress
Or gaze at her reflection in the mirror.

Then, without warning, the horror began.
The colour left her cheeks, and she staggered,
And would have fallen if one of her slaves
Had not offered her a chair. Her old nurse,
Thinking it was a god's frenzy, shouted
In triumph . . . until she saw the foam
Oozing from her lips, and the eyes rolling
In her bloodless face. Her cry of triumph
Changed to a wail of terror; the slave-girls
Scattered—one ran to fetch king Creon,
And another to tell Jason what had happened.
The rest ran up and down aimlessly,
Filling the whole palace with their sobs.

MEDEA:
    And Glauke? Did she die at once?

SERVANT:
                            At first
We thought so. For about the time it would take
A fast runner to reach the turning-post
And return to the start, she lay still.

137

Then, with a groan, she opened her eyes
And tried to sit up. It was horrible:
The crown was burning on her head, and the robe
Was eating into her flesh, destroying it.
Screaming, and blazing from head to foot,
She managed to get up at last, and shook
Her head, desperately trying to dislodge
The crown. But her efforts only fed the flames.
And at last, overcome with agony,
She collapsed on the floor again, and lay still.
No one but her father would have recognised her:
Her eyes had gone, and her cheeks and face
Were covered with a hideous oozing mess
Of blood and flames. The flesh dripped from her bones
Like pitch bubbling from a stricken pine-tree.
We were all too terrified to touch her,
Afraid of catching the plague ourselves.

MEDEA:

But you could see she was dead?

SERVANT:

She was dead all right: the poison had seen to that.
When Creon came in and saw what had happened,
He fell on her corpse like a madman, kissing it
And stroking it, trying to soothe her pain.
"My child," he sobbed, "why have the gods done this?
Why have they taken you from me—robbed me
Of an old man's only comfort? O Glauke,
Glauke my child, please let me die with you!"

His prayer was answered. When he tried to stand up,
His aged limbs clung to the bridal robe
As ivy clings to laurel-branches. He struggled,
And a terrible wrestling-match began,

138

The father trying to pull himself free,
And the daughter's corpse dragging him down
And tearing the living flesh from his bones.
At last he could fight no longer, and fell dead.
Now they lie there together, united in death,
The young bride and the father who loved her.
This is the fate the gods chose for them:
Man's life is no more than a fleeting shadow,
And even kings are not happy till they are dead.

CHORUS:

The gods have bestirred themselves today
And crushed Jason. We weep for you, Glauke
Daughter of Creon, princess of Corinth—
Yours has been a piteous wedding-day.

MEDEA:

My friends, my way is clear now.
I must kill the children,
And then hurry from Corinth.
I cannot let them live,
To suffer at my enemies' hands.
I gave them their life,
And I must take it away.
I will be strong, and do what must be done.
My whole life has been a preparation
For this moment, and I will live it to the end.
Be brave, Medea:
For this short day forget your sons—
You will have all eternity to mourn them.
I love them, and I must kill them . . .
Is anyone more accursed than I?

She hurries into the palace.

139

CHORUS:

O Sun, bright lord of heaven,
Look down on Medea, your daughter,
And the terrible crime she is planning.
The Furies are pressing her hard,
Urging her on to commit murder
And bring about her own destruction.

Why have the gods cursed you, Medea?
Why did they give you the blessing of sons?
Why did they bring you here to Corinth
Where that blessing became a curse?
There is no one on earth more miserable
Than a mother who kills her own children.

The CHILDREN's *voices are heard from inside,
terrified.*

PHERES:
Aah!
CHORUS:
Was that the children? O Medea,
How can you bear to kill them?
PHERES *from inside:*
Will no one help us?
Is there nowhere we can hide?
MERMEROS *from inside:*
Look! Our mother is coming,
Our own mother, coming to kill us!
CHORUS:
Shall we go in? Perhaps
There is still time to save them.
PHERES *inside:*
Help us! O Zeus, help us!

MERMEROS *inside:*

She is lifting the sword! Aah!

Silence.

CHORUS:

Unhappy Medea, is your heart a stone?
How could you bear to kill your own sons?

JASON *comes out of the palace, with armed* GUARDS
in attendance.

JASON:

Where is that viper Medea—out here
In the courtyard, or lurking in the palace?
Wherever she hides, she will not escape:
She can plunge deep into the Underworld,
Or take wing and soar up to Heaven itself,
But Creon's guards will still find her, and punish her
For destroying their master. She must die,
But my sons must be protected from harm—
Creon's kinsmen are angry, and will kill
Them with their mother, for the same crime,
Little caring who is innocent, and who guilty.

CHORUS:

Have you not heard what else has happened—
The latest tragedy? Have they not told you yet?

JASON:

What tragedy? Is she planning to kill me too?

CHORUS:

Your sons are dead—by their own mother's hand.

JASON:

Woman, what are you saying? My sons—dead?

CHORUS:

They are dead. Their brief hour of life is ended.

141

JASON:

Where did she kill them? Out here, or inside?

CHORUS:

Open the palace doors, and you will see.

JASON:

Guards! Quickly! Unbar the gates! Find their bodies—
And their murderess, whom I will repay with death!

The GUARDS *rush to the gates. But suddenly* MEDEA
*appears overhead in a chariot drawn by winged horses.
Her dead* CHILDREN *are at her feet.*

MEDEA:

I am here, Jason—here with your children.
If you have anything to say, say it now.

With a cry of fury, JASON *lunges at her with his
sword.*

You cannot reach me: my grandfather the Sun
Has given me this chariot to protect me,
And carry me out of your reach for ever.

JASON:

You viper! Do you dare ask the Sun to help you—
You, the woman who murdered her own sons
And left their father childless, the woman
Detested by the gods and the whole human race?
Why did I ever bring you here from Colchis?
I should have realised that a criminal
Who could betray her city and her own father
For my sake, would soon betray me too.
But the gods made me blind: I married you,
Cherishing in my heart the pestilence
That was to destroy my life, the tigress

Even the monsters of hell are afraid to look on!
But my scorn is wasted on you: your ears
Are too full of the screams of your victims
For words of mine to move you. Go, now—
You have left me nothing but misery;
I have no wife to cherish, no hopes of children.
You have destroyed me, Medea—go . . . go!

MEDEA:

I will not waste words answering you:
Zeus knows who is destroyer, and who destroyed.
You thought you could scorn our marriage,
Banish me from Corinth and forget me—
And you have been punished. Call me a viper,
A tigress, if you like—I have broken your heart
And taken the vengeance I longed for.

JASON:

And you have broken your own heart as well;
My grief is your grief too.

MEDEA:

                    My sons are dead;
Their father's tears are my only comfort.

JASON:

O my sons, how your mother hated you!

MEDEA:

No, my sons—your father's crimes destroyed you.

JASON:

My crimes? Was it my hand that killed them?

MEDEA:

No: it was your marriage, and your pride.

JASON:

My marriage? Is that why you killed them?

MEDEA:

What else could I have done?

143

JASON:

> You are insane . . .

MEDEA:

Your sons are dead—does that not move you?

JASON:

The gods will punish you.

MEDEA:

No: for they know who is really guilty.

JASON:

Is there no room in your heart for pity?

MEDEA:

None. I despise you, Jason.

JASON:

Well then, give me their bodies to bury,
And leave Corinth. I will not keep you here.

MEDEA:

No: I will bury my sons myself,
In Hera's shrine, where they will be safe
For ever from their enemies. King Aigeus
Has offered me sanctuary in Athens.
And as for you, Jason: the gods have chosen
A fitting death for you—a broken beam
From the wreckage of your precious *Argo*
Will fall on you one day and crush you.
And when that day comes, I will rejoice:
Our love, our marriage, will have come full circle.

JASON:

May the Furies destroy you
For what you have done—
And may avenging Justice . . .

MEDEA:

Why should the gods listen to you?
You broke your oaths

And cheated those you loved.

JASON:

But it was not I who killed my own sons.

MEDEA *with scorn:*

Go inside.

Go in and bury your wife.

JASON:

My wife and sons are dead;

I have nothing left.

MEDEA:

You will feel it more when you are old,

And there is no one to comfort you.

JASON:

O my children!

MEDEA:

Their mother loved them, not you.

JASON:

Loved them—and killed them?

MEDEA:

I killed them to punish you.

JASON:

Let me touch them again!

Let me kiss them,

And caress them for the last time!

MEDEA:

No. You turned them away before:

Why should you embrace them now?

JASON:

Medea, I beg you, let me touch them—

MEDEA:

No. You are wasting your breath.

JASON:

O Zeus! Can you not hear her?

She has murdered her own children,
And still will not let me touch them!
I will mourn them for ever.
Mourn for the sons I begot
For their own mother to kill!

CHORUS:
High overhead, in Olympos,
Lord Zeus looks after the affairs of men.
The gods follow no laws but their own:
What men hope for never happens,
And what they least expect occurs
By the will of heaven. So it was
With what has happened here.

THE FROGS

NOTE

The Frogs must surely be one of the first "black comedies" ever written. The idea of sending Dionysos, god of drama, down to hell to bring back a worthwhile dramatist, and the resulting by-play with corpses, hideous monsters and the inhabitants of the underworld, bring it very close to the "sick humour" of our own day. It was first produced in 405 B.C., and was an immediate success. The parabasis (p. 177) was so well liked that the play was given the unusual honour of an immediate second performance.

In many ways this first production marked the end of an era. Both Euripides and Sophocles had recently died, and there was no one left to continue the great tradition of Greek tragedy. The Peloponnesian War, too, which had overshadowed Athenian life for a generation, was at last drawing to a close.

Even comedy was changing. "Old Comedy", with its savage satire and heavy reliance on the Chorus, was beginning to incorporate elements of what became "New Comedy" thirty years later. The role of the Chorus is less important; the plot is more complicated and "bitty", and minor characters (like Xanthias and the Porter) are given parts far bigger than their importance demands.

Where *The Frogs* keeps closest to the style of Old Comedy is in the poetical contest with which it ends. This is one of the very few pieces of literary criticism that have survived from Aristophanes' own time, and it is interesting to compare his comments on Aeschylus and Euripides with what we know of their work today. Clearly the points he makes are exaggerated for comic effect; but there is a grain of truth even in Dionysos' most ludicrous comments (e.g., in the

148

weighing scene, p. 198). Obviously, too, he must have had great respect for his victims—his attacks on Euripides, in this and other plays, reveal a detailed knowledge of the tragedies one would hardly expect if he disliked them as much as he pretends.

But the literary criticism comes later on. The play opens in a street in Athens, with a conversation between Dionysos and Xanthias that has set the pattern for almost every comedy double act since . . .

THE FROGS

Characters in order of appearance:
DIONYSOS, the god of poetry
XANTHIAS, his slave
HERAKLES
A CORPSE
CHARON, a ferryman
PORTER at the palace of King Pluto
SERVING-MAID
LANDLADY
PLATHANE, her friend
PLUTO, the king of the underworld
EURIPIDES ⎫ tragic dramatists
AESCHYLUS ⎭
CHORUS of FROGS
CHORUS of the HOLY ONES

Undertakers' men, slaves, musicians, dancing-girls, the Dead, etc.

THE FROGS

SCENE ONE

The street outside HERAKLES' *house, with a path leading down to the lakeside.* DIONYSOS *comes in wearing a yellow costume covered by a lion-skin, and carrying a club. His slave* XANTHIAS *follows, riding on a donkey, and loaded with baggage.*

XANTHIAS: Go on, sir, let's start with one of the old jokes they always laugh at.

DIONYSOS: All right . . . so long as it's not "I'm crushed to death!" We'd never get away with that.

XANTHIAS: There are plenty of better ones.

DIONYSOS: Yes, but not "I've really had it!"

XANTHIAS: Well, what about . . .

DIONYSOS *quickly*: No, no!

XANTHIAS: What?

DIONYSOS: Not the one where you keep shifting your bags about, and then suddenly shout: "I've got to ease myself!"

XANTHIAS: Not even "Hold these for a moment, while I . . ."?

DIONYSOS: Not unless you want me to be sick.

XANTHIAS: I dunno. What's the point of me carrying all these bags if I can't get a laugh out of them? They all do it, you know . . . Phrynichos, Lykis, Ameipsias . . . there's a baggage scene in every comedy.

DIONYSOS: But not in this one. Leave that sort of thing to Phrynichos and Ameipsias . . . I come away from their plays a year older as it is.

XANTHIAS: Poor old shoulders! *Crushed to death* they are—and that's no joke!

DIONYSOS: The whole thing's no joke. Here am I, Dionysos son of Juice, wandering about on foot like a beggar, and letting you ride the donkey, just to save you carrying a few little bags.

XANTHIAS: You mean I'm *not* carrying them?

DIONYSOS: You, carrying them? You're riding the donkey.

XANTHIAS: I tell you I'm bearing the baggage.

DIONYSOS: How d'you mean, bearing it?

XANTHIAS: Grin-and-bearing it!

DIONYSOS: How can someone bear something, when someone else is bearing him?

XANTHIAS: Oh, I don't know. All I know is, I *want to ease myself*!

DIONYSOS: Well, ease yourself off that donkey, if he isn't doing you any good. We're here anyway . . . this is Herakles' house. Just a minute . . . I'll knock. Hello inside! Anybody in?

He hammers on the door with his club. HERAKLES *answers it crossly.*

HERAKLES: What are you trying to do, hammer the door down? *(astounded)* My god! What is it?

He props himself against the doorway, laughing help-lessly.

DIONYSOS *aside to* XANTHIAS: There, you see.

XANTHIAS: What?

DIONYSOS: He's terrified.

XANTHIAS: Terrified you've gone crazy, you mean.

HERAKLES: It's no good . . . I can't help it . . . it's ridiculous . . .

DIONYSOS: Come over here, my dear chap. Don't be afraid. I've something to ask you.

151

HERAKLES: Why the lion-skin and the tragic robe? Why
   . . . why the *club*? (*controlling himself with an effort*) Er
   . . . yes . . . who are you, my friend? Just back from a
   battle?
   He collapses in helpless laughter again.
DIONYSOS *with dignity:* I've been at sea . . . with
   Kleisthenes.
HERAKLES: Oh yes? At the battle?
DIONYSOS: As a matter of fact, yes. We sank twelve or
   thirteen of the enemy, too.
HERAKLES: I don't believe it.
DIONYSOS: Ask anyone.
XANTHIAS: Then we woke up . . .
DIONYSOS *flashing him a look of hatred:* But the point is,
   while I was on the ship, reading Euripides' *Andromeda*,
   I had a sudden desire . . .
HERAKLES: Oh? How big?
DIONYSOS: About this big . . .
HERAKLES: For a woman?
DIONYSOS: No, no.
HERAKLES: A boy, then?
DIONYSOS: No.
HERAKLES: A man?
DIONYSOS: Good heavens, no.
HERAKLES: Surely not for *Kleisthenes*!
DIONYSOS: It's not a joking matter. It's eating me away.
HERAKLES: There, there . . . What are the symptoms?
DIONYSOS: It's not easy to explain. How can I put
   it . . . ? Ah! I know! Have you ever had a sudden
   longing for pea-soup?
HERAKLES: Pea-soup? Do I ever long for anything else?
DIONYSOS: Is that clear, or shall I try again?
HERAKLES: No, no . . . pea-soup's clear enough . . . if

you see what I mean.

DIONYSOS: Well, it's that sort of longing that's eating me up . . . for Euripides.

HERAKLES: Euripides? Ergh! He's a *corpse*!

DIONYSOS: I'm still going to see him, and no one's going to stop me.

HERAKLES: You mean, down to hell?

DIONYSOS: Lower, if necessary.

HERAKLES: But *why*?

DIONYSOS: I need to talk to a decent poet. There aren't any left, now he's dead . . . nothing but rubbish.

HERAKLES: What d'you mean? There's Iophon.

DIONYSOS: Not my cup of tea at all.

HERAKLES: Well, if you must see someone, why not Sophocles? He's far better than Euripides.

DIONYSOS: Ah! But I want to bring someone back. I'd never persuade Sophocles to come with me: he likes an easy life . . . and an easy death, come to that. But Euripides'll slip away like a shot.

HERAKLES: Hey! What's wrong with Agathon?

DIONYSOS: Gone, poor chap. Shuffled off.

HERAKLES: Shuffled off where?

DIONYSOS: Down Below . . . the Banquets of the Blessed.

HERAKLES: Well, what about Xenokles?

DIONYSOS: To hell with him!

HERAKLES: Or Pythangelos?

XANTHIAS *aside*: What about me? My shoulder's *really* had it.

HERAKLES: There must be thousands of playwrights still around . . . miles more wordy than Euripides.

DIONYSOS: Barren leaves . . . dregs . . . chattering starlings. They get one play put on, cock their legs once

153

at Tragedy, and you never hear of them again. No no, I want a *real* poet, one who isn't afraid of a bit of language.

HERAKLES: How d'you mean?

DIONYSOS: Surely you remember those phrases Euripides was so good at . . . "Air, Zeus's mansion" . . . or "The foot of time" . . . or "My tongue it was that promised, not my brain."

HERAKLES *surprised*: You like that sort of thing?

DIONYSOS: I'm mad about it.

HERAKLES: But it's a load of old . . .

DIONYSOS: Now, now.

HERAKLES: Well, I mean . . .

DIONYSOS: Look, I don't lecture you about food, do I?

XANTHIAS *aside*: Have they forgotten I exist?

DIONYSOS: Anyway, I came to see you because you've been *down* there . . . the time you went to steal Cerberus. I want you to tell me all you can about the place . . . harbours, bread-shops, pubs, water-holes, cities, landladies, doss-houses with the least bugs . . .

XANTHIAS *aside*: After all, I *am* still here.

HERAKLES: You fool! You're not planning to go there *really*?

DIONYSOS: Of course I am. Just tell me the quickest way down . . . and don't make it too hot or too cold, either.

HERAKLES: H'm, let me see . . . There's the Block and Tackle way.

DIONYSOS: Eh?

HERAKLES: Hanging yourself.

DIONYSOS: No, no . . . I'd choke to death!

HERAKLES: What about the Pestle and Mortar way?

DIONYSOS: Hemlock, you mean?

HERAKLES: That's right.

154

DIONYSOS: Now you're trying to give me cold feet.

HERAKLES: You want a quick, short way, don't you?

DIONYSOS: That's it. I'm not much of a walker.

HERAKLES: All right. Straight up the road . . turn left into Potters Row . . .

DIONYSOS: Then what?

HERAKLES: Climb to the top of the tower.

DIONYSOS: Eh? Whatever for?

HERAKLES: Wait till they start the torch-race . . . and when you hear them shouting: "They're off!", you be off as well.

DIONYSOS: Off? Where?

HERAKLES: Down.

DIONYSOS: No thanks. D'you *want* me to lose my head? What about the road you took?

HERAKLES: Ah, that depends. Do you get seasick?

DIONYSOS: No. Why?

HERAKLES: There's a lot of water involved. First, you come to a vast bottomless lake.

DIONYSOS: How do I get across?

HERAKLES: There's an aged ferryman . . .

DIONYSOS: Ah! you mean Charon.

HERAKLES: That's right. He'll take you over, for two silver pieces.

DIONYSOS: I thought the fare was one silver piece.

HERAKLES: But you want a *return* ticket, don't you?

DIONYSOS: I see.

HERAKLES: Once you get to the other side, past all the snakes and monsters . . .

DIONYSOS: You're trying to put me off, aren't you?

HERAKLES: . . . you'll come to the Mud Marsh and the Great Desolation of Dung. That's where they keep people who cheated their friends, or beat up their mothers, or

155

thumped their fathers, or swore false oaths . . .

DIONYSOS: Or learned poems by Morsimos, or tried their hand at Kinesias' torch-dance . . .

HERAKLES: Then suddenly there'll be a breath of flutes, and everything'll turn bright and sunny, like it is up here. That means you've reached the Myrtle Groves, and the Banquets of the Blessed . . . men and women feasting, clapping their hands, dancing . . .

DIONYSOS: Who are they?

HERAKLES: The Holy Ones, who understand the Mysteries.

XANTHIAS *aside:* I wish I understood the mystery of why I'm still carrying this lot!

HERAKLES: They'll answer all your questions, and put you right, on the road to Pluto's palace. Well, the best of luck . . .

DIONYSOS: And to you, my dear fellow.

HERAKLES *goes in and shuts the door.*

Come on, Xanthias, pick up the bags.

XANTHIAS: Have I ever put them down?

DIONYSOS: Don't argue. Hurry up.

XANTHIAS: Shh! Look!

A funeral procession comes down the street.

Can't you get *him* to carry them? Save me coming at all.

DIONYSOS: What if he says no?

XANTHIAS: I'll have no choice then, will I?

DIONYSOS: All right. (*shouting*) I say, just a minute . . . Mr Corpse . . .

The procession stops, and the CORPSE *sits up crossly.*

CORPSE: Yes?

DIONYSOS: Going down to hell, are you?

CORPSE: What do *you* think?

DIONYSOS: Well, I wonder if you'd do me a favour . . .
a few bags to take down . . .

CORPSE: Where are they?

DIONYSOS: Here.

CORPSE: That lot? It'll cost you two drachmas.

DIONYSOS: Oh come on, be reasonable.

CORPSE *to the undertakers*: On we go!

DIONYSOS: No no, just a minute. Can't we come to some
arrangement?

CORPSE: Two drachmas, or nothing doing.

DIONYSOS: One and a half . . .

CORPSE: Do me a favour . . . I'd rather live!

He signs to the undertakers, who carry him out.

XANTHIAS: Cheeky beggar! He'll be sorry, one day. Oh
well, I suppose I'd better come.

DIONYSOS *sarcastically*: I don't know what I'd do without
you. Now, let's see if we can find that ferryboat . . .

*They walk round the stage. Gradually it gets darker.
Suddenly* CHARON *looms up ahead, waiting at a jetty
by the lakeside.*

CHARON: Avast behind!

DIONYSOS *offended*: Pardon?

XANTHIAS: This is it, sir. The lake he told us about, and
the ferryman. What's his name? Charon.

DIONYSOS: Hi there, Charon! Nice day for a sail . . .

CHARON *ignoring him*: Any more for the Dogs, the Ground
Floor, the Lower Depths, or the Last Resting Place?

DIONYSOS: Yes, me.

CHARON: Get in, then, quick.

DIONYSOS: This is the right way to go to hell?

CHARON *grimly*: You can say that again. Get in, can't you?

DIONYSOS: After you, Xanthias.

CHARON: No no—no slaves allowed. Unless they served

157

at sea, of course.

XANTHIAS: Ah! I was exempt . . . bad eyesight, you know.

CHARON: Well, you'll have to walk . . . all the way round the lake.

XANTHIAS: Where shall I meet you?

CHARON: At the Skull and Skeletons . . . the pub by the Withered Rock.

XANTHIAS *gloomily:* I see. What a way to earn a living!
He goes off, groping in the shadows.

CHARON: Right, you. Sit to your oar. (*shouting*) Anyone else? Any more for the die-lark? (*To* DIONYSOS) Now what are you doing?

DIONYSOS: Sitting on my oar. That's what you said, isn't it?

CHARON *angrily:* You great lumbering . . . (*controlling himself*). Here, sit there.

DIONYSOS *nervously:* All right.

CHARON: Stick your hand out.

DIONYSOS: There.

CHARON: Grab hold of this.

DIONYSOS: Like that?

CHARON: Now, stop fooling about, and PULL!

DIONYSOS: Pull . . . me? I've never rowed a boat before. Which end do you hold?

CHARON: It's simple, once you get going. The frog-swans will sing to you, and help you along.

DIONYSOS: Who?

CHARON: Frog-swans . . . you'll see. Are you ready?

DIONYSOS: I suppose so.

CHARON: All right. ONE-two three, ONE-two-three . . .

DIONYSOS *starts rowing to this rhythm. The boat moves across the stage in the darkness. The air gradually fills with the sound of the* FROGS. *Their song is in an entirely different rhythm from the rowing, and puts* DIONYSOS *completely off his stroke.*

FROGS:

    Brekekekex, koax, koax,
    Brekekekex, koax, koax,
    Children of the limpid lakes,
    Sing with us, till the echo breaks
    Along the reedbeds by the shore.
    Sing as you never sang before,
    For Dionysos, Lord of the Vine,
    Who leads the singing and laughter
    As the revellers dance in the shrine
    And then stagger home, the morning after—
    Brekekekex, koax, koax.

DIONYSOS:

    I'm getting a blistered behind,
    Brekekekex, koax, koax;
    Stop singing . . . do you mind?

FROGS:

    Brekekekex, koax, koax.

DIONYSOS:

    Oh, go to hell with your koax!
    Is that all you can say, koax?

FROGS:

    In deep dark pools where fat carp feed
    We plant and raise the sacred reed
    For Apollo's lute. The Muses hymn us,
    Expert divers, expert swimmers,
    For the sweetness of our singing.
    All nature runs, its trophies bringing,
    To join with us in the dance of Pan
    In honour of *you*, you ungrateful man!

Brekekekex, koax, koax.

DIONYSOS:

I don't care. I'm getting quite sore,
Brekekekex, koax, koax;
And my behind's getting ready to roar—

FROGS:

Brekekekex, koax, koax.

DIONYSOS:

I've had enough. Please stop your song.
It's really gone on a bit too long.

FROGS:

No! How could we possibly? Please
Don't ask us again to cease.
We sang all summer, while sunny days
Warmed the swamps, and our praise
Rose to heaven. And now, in the rain,
Our burbling, gurgling refrain
Rises up in honour of you,
With its bubbling echo bursting through:
Brekekekex, koax, koax.

DIONYSOS:

It's my turn now, kekekex, koax;
So stop your row, kekekex, koax!

FROGS:

No no, please don't, kekekex, koax;
Please say you won't, kekekex, koax.

DIONYSOS:

I tell you I've had enough of you . . .
And I've nearly rowed myself in two!

FROGS:

Brekekekex, koax, koax.

DIONYSOS:

Please stop it; you're driving me mad.

160

FROGS:

    Oh dear, that would really be sad.
    We'll never give up; till the end of the day
    We'll warble on in our frogular way,
    Brekekekex, koax, koax.

DIONYSOS:

    I'll crush your koagular vein!
    Fancy rowing a boat, in the rain,
    Through desolate marshes and bogs,
    Swapping songs with a chorus of frogs!
    Brekekekex, koax, koax.

FROGS:

    You'll never win: it's our turn now.

DIONYSOS:

    I'll win all right. I'll show you how:
    I won't give up, I'll yell myself hoarse;
    I'll stop your koax, if need be by force—
    Brekekekex, koax . . . KOAX!
    Silence.
    No answer? You've gone away?
    I knew in the end I'd win the day.

CHARON: All right, stop rowing. We're here. Ship the oars
    and step ashore. Fares, please.

DIONYSOS: Here you are.

    He hands CHARON *the fare, and steps ashore. The
    boat disappears into the gloom.* DIONYSOS *gropes about
    in the darkness, in mounting terror.*
    Xanthias? Xanthias? Wh-where are you? Xan-thi-as!

XANTHIAS *appearing suddenly from behind a rock:* Boo!

DIONYSOS *startled:* Aah! (*recovering himself*) Come over
    here.

XANTHIAS: Welcome to hell, sir.

DIONYSOS: Wh-what's over that way?

161

XANTHIAS: Mud . . . darkness . . .

DIONYSOS: Did you see any of the murderers and oath-breakers he told us about?

XANTHIAS *pointing to the audience*: There. Hundreds of 'em.

DIONYSOS: Oh yes. Well, what next?

XANTHIAS: I think we'd better move on. This is where all the monsters are—or so Herakles said.

DIONYSOS: You don't mean to say you believed him? He was piling it on, trying to frighten me—*me*, the bravest god in Greece! Typical Herakles, that . . . he's just jealous. I wouldn't mind meeting a monster right now . . . a fight would really tone up my muscles for the rest of the trip.

XANTHIAS *suddenly*: Shh! What was that?

DIONYSOS *terrified*: What? Where?

XANTHIAS: Behind you.

DIONYSOS *pushing him behind*: Get over there.

XANTHIAS: Now it's in front.

DIONYSOS *pushing him in front*: Over *there*, I said.

XANTHIAS *with a cry of mock terror*: Aah!

DIONYSOS: Wh-wh-what?

XANTHIAS: I can see a huge great beast.

DIONYSIS: Wh-what's it like?

XANTHIAS: Oh, horrible. It keeps changing. Now it's a cow . . . now it's a mule. Ooh! Now it's a pretty young girl . . .

DIONYSOS: Where? Where? Let's have a look.

XANTHIAS: Too late. It's changed again. Now it's a she-wolf.

DIONYSOS: It must be Empousa. Is one leg made of copper?

XANTHIAS: Just a minute . . . yes. And one of cow-dung.

DIONYSOS *terrified:* Ooh! Where can I hide?

He runs wildly about the stage.

XANTHIAS: Hey! Don't leave me behind!

DIONYSOS: Save me, prompter, save me . . . don't forget I owe you a drink.

XANTHIAS: We're done for, Herakles.

DIONYSOS: Shh! Don't call me that down here!

XANTHIAS: Dionysos, then.

DIONYSOS: That's even worse.

XANTHIAS *to the non-existent monster:* Shoo! Shoo! Bad girl! Shoo! (*to* DIONYSOS) It's all right, sir. This way.

DIONYSOS: What d'you mean?

XANTHIAS: Empousa's hopped it.

DIONYSOS: You're joking.

XANTHIAS: No, no.

DIONYSOS: Swear.

XANTHIAS: By Zeus.

DIONYSOS: You really mean it?

XANTHIAS: Really.

DIONYSOS: Phew! D'you know, I went quite pale for a moment.

XANTHIAS: *You* went pale? You should see the prompter!

DIONYSOS: It was quite nasty, I can tell you. I wonder which of the gods she came from? "Air, Zeus's mansion", or "The Foot of Time"?

XANTHIAS: Shh!

DIONYSOS *terrified:* Oh no! Not another one!

XANTHIAS: No, no. Can't you hear it?

DIONYSOS: What?

XANTHIAS: A breath of flutes.

DIONYSOS: Oh yes . . . and a whiff of torches. It must be a procession. Quick, come over here. Get your

163

head down . . . we don't want them to see us.

CHORUS *off*:

Iacchos, O Iacchos!

Iacchos, O Iacchos!

XANTHIAS: It must be the Holy Ones . . . the procession from the Mysteries.

DIONYSOS: Shh! Keep quiet, and we'll see.

They crouch down, as the CHORUS *come in in procession, wearing garlands and carrying blazing torches.*

CHORUS:

Iacchos, O Iacchos!

Lord of these holy places, lead the dance

As the Blessed Ones across the fields advance;

Come down and crown our feast, O lord, we pray;

Come down and honour us on this holy day.

XANTHIAS:

Demeter! What a lovely smell of pork!

DIONYSOS:

Shh! Keep quiet, and you'll get a bit of sausage.

CHORUS:

Iacchos, O Iacchos!

Come down, O morning star, and end the night;

Come down, till the plain is filled with light,

And old men throw away their crutches and come

To dance. Come down, O lord! Bring joy to everyone!

LEADER:

Some men have no time for our rites:

They've no use at all for the dance

Of the Muses, and won't spend their nights

In a ritual, bacchanal prance

To the songs of Kratinos; they hate

Any pleasure that keeps them up late

CHORUS:

Iacchos, O Iacchos,
Keep them away from our festival!

LEADER:

Some men, when they go to a play,
Hate all but the dirtiest joke;
And some politicians today
Make speeches that quickly provoke
Demonstrations and riots, and send
Decent citizens quite round the bend.

CHORUS:

Iacchos, O Iacchos,
Keep them away from our festival!

LEADER:

Some men take the enemy's pay
To ruin the city; some implore us
To pardon their second-rate play;
Some, when a comedy chorus
Makes fun of them, cut down my fee—
Pure meanness, I think you'll agree.

CHORUS:

Iacchos, O Iacchos,
Keep them away from our festival!

LEADER:

Forward, then, into the fields,
To laugh and dance and sing
The praise of the maiden goddess
Who brought us back the spring.

CHORUS:

Iacchos, lord of the dance, come down to us now!

LEADER:

Lady Demeter, hear our prayer;
As our songs to heaven rise

Look on our play with favour,
And let it win first prize.

CHORUS:

Iacchos, lord of the dance, come down to us now!

They start to move off. DIONYSOS *gets up hurriedly.*

DIONYSOS: Er . . . I say . . .

LEADER: Iacchos, lord . . . Yes, what is it?

DIONYSOS: I wonder if you could tell me the way to Pluto's palace. We're strangers in these parts . . .

LEADER: Just up the road . . . first palace on the left.

DIONYSOS: Thank you so much. Come on, Xanthias, pick up the bags.

XANTHIAS *bitterly:* "Xanthias, pick up the bags"—that's all you ever say!

CHORUS *as they go:*

The rose-meadows are waiting, lord Iacchos—come
And we will honour you, warmed by the sun
That only the Blessed know, the sacred flame
Enjoyed by all who worship Justice' name.
Iacchos, lord of the dance, come down to us now.

As they process out of sight, the stage lights up, revealing the imposing door of Pluto's palace.

DIONYSOS: Ah! Here we are . . . Pluto's palace. Now, what's the best way to knock, d'you think? I wonder how they knock on doors in these parts.

XANTHIAS: Oh, get on with it! Any way you like . . . only don't forget you're supposed to be Herakles.

DIONYSOS: Right. (*hammering on the door with his club*) All right, you lot! Anyone in?

The PORTER, *a sergeant-major type, opens the door fiercely.*

PORTER: 'Oo is it?

DIONYSOS: Herakles the Strong.

PORTER: Ho, it's you, is it? You horrible little man, thought you'd come back and see how we was doing, did you? AND STAND UP STRAIGHT WHEN I'M TALKING TO YOU! Runs off with Cerberus, then comes back to laugh at us! A right little joker—AND GET YOUR HAIR CUT! Well, I've got news for you. We've been waiting for you. Tithrasian gorgons'll 'ave you, sharpish, AND I wouldn't like to be you when they've finished with you. You'll be on tortures so long, you won't remember what it was like not to feel the pincers . . . WHAT WAS THAT? You got anything to say, my lad, you keep quiet about it, or I'll have you . . . I'll 'ave you as far as Tartaros and back . . .

DIONYSOS: But . . .

PORTER: WAIT FOR IT! I'll tell you when to speak!

He goes. DIONYSOS *slumps.*

XANTHIAS: Sir, sir! What's the matter?

DIONYSOS: I've . . . er . . . had an accident.

XANTHIAS: Why don't you clear off while you've got the chance?

DIONYSOS *in anguish:* You don't understand . . . I've had an *accident.* Give me a sponge, quick.

XANTHIAS: Where d'you want it?

DIONYSOS: Put it on my heart. There.

XANTHIAS: Good lord! Is *that* where you keep your heart?

DIONYSOS: It . . . er . . . slipped a bit in the excitement.

XANTHIAS: A right little Herakles *you* are!

DIONYSOS: What d'you mean? I asked for a sponge, didn't I? How many men would have kept their heads

167

and asked for a sponge?

XANTHIAS: You're joking.

DIONYSOS: Well, weren't *you* afraid? All that shouting!

XANTHIAS *airily*: Me? No. Hot air, all of it.

DIONYSOS: All right, if you're so brave, change clothes with me.

XANTHIAS: What?

DIONYSOS: Pick up the club and put on the lion-skin. I'll be you, and carry the bags.

XANTHIAS: All right, I don't see why not. (*As they change clothes*) After all, it's not every day you see a Heraklio-xanthias. I bet I do it better than you, too.

DIONYSOS: All right, all right, don't go on. Now, the bags . . . Golly! They're quite a weight, aren't they?

He is reluctant to pick them up, but the sound of a key in the lock makes him grab them hastily and duck out of sight. XANTHIAS *braces himself—but instead of the* PORTER *a beautiful* SERVING-MAID *comes out.*

MAID: Herakles, darling! You've come back at last! We could hardly believe our ears in the kitchen. They've put the peas on and started chopping up the carrots . . . there's a whole ox for dinner tonight. And you should *see* the cakes they're baking you! Come on in . . .

XANTHIAS: No, no . . . really . . .

MAID: Oh, come on. There's pigeon pie, and lamb stew, and we've opened a keg of Pluto's best wine. Come in, there's a darling . . .

XANTHIAS: Well, I . . .

MAID: I won't let you slip away this time. We've hired a flute-girl in your honour, and two or three dancing-girls.

XANTHIAS: What was that? Dancing-girls?

MAID: That's right . . . young and pretty. Come inside.
   The table's laid, and everything's ready.
XANTHIAS: All right. Go and tell the dancing-girls I'll
   be in shortly . . . in person.

   The MAID *goes in, and he turns to* DIONYSOS.

   Hey you! Pick up the bags, and follow me.
DIONYSOS: Just a minute, just a minute. You surely
   didn't take me seriously just now?
XANTHIAS: What? When?
DIONYSOS: When I asked you to dress up as Herakles.
XANTHIAS: Eh?
DIONYSOS: Pick up the bags, and stop messing about.
XANTHIAS: You're not trying to make me change back,
   are you?
DIONYSOS: I certainly am. Take off that lion-skin.
XANTHIAS: Ye gods . . .
DIONYSOS: Precisely. Have you forgotten who I am?
   And who *you* are? Take off that skin.
XANTHIAS: Oh, all right. But we'll see who laughs last.

   They struggle into each other's clothes again.

CHORUS *meanwhile:*
   What a clever idea:
   When danger is near,
   To roll with the ship and avoid it!
   Adapt your position
   Like a shrewd politician;
   Don't wait till events have destroyed it!
DIONYSOS:
   Yes: for I won't have it said
   That my slave lay in bed
   Having fun with a flute-girl beside him,

169

While I ran about
Like an idiot lout
Looking on at the goodies denied him!

He is so busy changing he doesn't notice the LANDLADY *and* PLATHANE *coming up the road behind him.*

LANDLADY: Good lord, Plathane, it's him. The swine who stayed in our hotel, and ate eleven loaves at a single sitting!

PLATHANE: You're right! It *is* him!

DIONYSOS: Erk!

XANTHIAS *aside:* I'm going to enjoy this.

LANDLADY: And twenty portions of roast lamb at a drachma each.

XANTHIAS *aside:* It's going to be good.

PLATHANE: And all those onions!

DIONYSOS *nervously:* Ridiculous, madam! You don't know what you're talking about.

LANDLADY: I suppose you thought I wouldn't recognise you with that yellow dress on. I haven't even *mentioned* the cheese!

PLATHANE: A hundredweight of best mousetrap . . . rind and all!

LANDLADY: And when I tried to give him the bill, he twitched his eyebrows at me and went "BOO!"

XANTHIAS: Oh, he's like that. Does it all the time.

LANDLADY: Then he pulled out his sword like a maniac . . . chased me upstairs and locked me in the . . . well, *you* know. Then he hopped it, taking half the carpet with him.

XANTHIAS: That's him all over.

PLATHANE: What are we going to do with him?

LANDLADY: Get a sickle, and cut the throat that in!

PLATHANE: Throw him over the cliff!

LANDLADY: Get a sickle, and cut the throat that demolished all our beetroot!

PLATHANE: Come on! Let's go for the police!

They hurry out. There is a long pause.

DIONYSOS: Er . . . Xanthias . . .

XANTHIAS: No! It's no use. I'm not playing Herakles again.

DIONYSOS: Oh, go on . . . Xanthy . . .

XANTHIAS: Have you forgotten who I am? And who *you* are?

DIONYSOS: You're quite right to be angry . . . hit me if you like, I won't blame you. But it's such a lovely lion-skin . . . and I promise not to ask for it back . . . ever. I swear it.

XANTHIAS *wavering*: We-e-ell . . .

DIONYSOS: Cross my heart and hope to die.

XANTHIAS: Oh, all right.

They change clothes again.

CHORUS:
Now you're back in the part
That you had at the start,
You must screw up your eyebrows and roar;
You must act like a god,
And do nothing odd,
Or you'll end up far worse than before.

XANTHIAS:
I'm sure I agree.
But the trouble, you see,
Is: my master's a trembling coward.

There is a crash from inside the palace.

Hey! What was that noise?
The porter and his boys!
Now I must roar, long and . . . er . . . loward!

He braces himself. The PORTER *comes out with two* SLAVES.

PORTER: There's the dognapper! Grab him, quick!

DIONYSOS *aside:* Someone's for it now.

XANTHIAS *loudly:* Keep back! I warn you . . .

PORTER: Oho! Smasher . . . Nabber . . . Grabber . . . come out here, quickly!

DIONYSOS *airily, to no one in particular:* Fantastic, isn't it? Steals what doesn't belong to him, then hits a policeman.

PORTER: Unbelievable.

DIONYSOS: Worse: incredible.

XANTHIAS: Look, I've never been here before in my life. I've never stolen so much as a hair off your head! May I go to hell if I have. I'll make you a fair offer: take my slave, and torture him. *Then* if you find I'm guilty, you can do what you like with me.

PORTER: Torture him, eh? How would you suggest?

XANTHIAS: Oh, any way you like . . . rack, thumbscrews, whips, vinegar up the nose, bricks on the chest . . . anything except beating him with leeks or rubbing him with raw onion.

PORTER: You can't say fairer than that. But what if I . . . *break* him a little? You won't want damages, will you?

XANTHIAS *wiping his eyes with laughter:* Damages! That's a good one! No, no: take him away, and do what you like with him.

PORTER: Take him away? No, I'll do it here, where you can see fair play. (to DIONYSOS) Hey you, come out from behind those bags. We'll get the truth out of you, even if it kills you.

DIONYSOS: Er . . . no! No . . . I forbid it.

PORTER: Pardon?

DIONYSOS: I'm a god, and I won't have it.

PORTER: Eh?

DIONYSOS: Just touch me . . . you'll be sorry.

PORTER: What?

DIONYSOS: I'm Dionysos, son of Zeus. He's the slave.

PORTER to XANTHIAS: Did you hear that?

XANTHIAS: I certainly did. All the more reason for torturing him.

PORTER: Why?

XANTHIAS: If he's a god, he won't feel it.

DIONYSOS with sudden inspiration: Just a minute! You say you're a god . . . Why don't you let him whip you, too?

XANTHIAS: Fair enough.

DIONYSOS taken aback: Blow for blow?

XANTHIAS: Blow for blow—and the first to scream or show any sign of pain, isn't a god.

PORTER: You mean that?

XANTHIAS: I mean it.

PORTER: You are a gent. I can always tell. All right, take your shirts off.

XANTHIAS takes off his shirt, and DIONYSOS follows less willingly. The PORTER picks up a large whip, and flexes his muscles.

XANTHIAS: Right.

The PORTER hits him.

173

PORTER: There.

XANTHIAS: Ready when you are.

PORTER: I've just hit you.

XANTHIAS: You're joking.

PORTER: I see. Now *this* one.

He hits DIONYSOS.

DIONYSOS: Come on, then.

PORTER: I've just hit you.

DIONYSOS: Nonsense! I'd have felt the draught.

PORTER: I dunno . . . I'd better try the other one again.

XANTHIAS: Fair enough.

The PORTER *hits him, hard.*

Crrrrikey!

PORTER: What d'you mean, crrrrikey? Felt that, did you?

XANTHIAS: No, no. I was just thinking that the Festival will be starting any minute now, and I'm going to be late.

PORTER: The man's a saint! Back to this one . . .

He hits DIONYSOS.

DIONYSOS: Ooh! Ooh!

PORTER: What's the matter?

DIONYSOS: Look, a procession!

PORTER: What are you crying for?

DIONYSOS: Can't *you* smell onions?

PORTER: Are you *sure* you didn't feel anything?

DIONYSOS *airily:* Not a thing.

PORTER: Right. Back to Herakles.

He whips XANTHIAS *again.*

XANTHIAS: Oh! Oho-oh-oh!

PORTER: Ah! What's the matter?

XANTHIAS: Thorn in my foot.

PORTER: I don't get this. Back to the other one . . .

He hits DIONYSOS *again.*

DIONYSOS: My god! Er . . . "I love thee, not because . . ."

XANTHIAS: He felt that all right. Didn't you hear?

DIONYSOS: No, no. How does that hymn go? ". . . not because I hope for heaven thereby . . ."?

XANTHIAS: We're getting nowhere. Hit him lower down.

PORTER: Oi! Stick your belly out.

He hits DIONYSOS'S *stomach.*

DIONYSOS: Poseidon!

XANTHIAS: Aha!

DIONYSOS: "Who rules the stormy waves by th'Aegean's beetling crag . . ."

PORTER: Oh, this is ridiculous. I can't tell which one of you's the god. You'd better both come inside . . . the master'll know . . . and Queen Persephone. After all, they're gods themselves.

DIONYSOS: All right. But I wish you'd thought of it sooner . . .

They go in, DIONYSOS *and* XANTHIAS *limping slightly.*

CHORUS:
　　O sacred Muse of comedy,
　　Can't you see how eagerly
　　The audience are waiting?
　　Come down and bless our festival;
　　Smile on us; grant us your favour.

LEADER:
　　It's perfectly right to break into a play
　　Of this type with some serious moments, and give
　　You some useful advice. So our theme for today

175

Is a simple one: "Live and let live."
For surely it's clear that the state's in a mess,
When a man who is honest and decent and brave
Has to drag out his life in disgrace and distress
For being over fifty—although any slave
Who helped us in battle is rightly rewarded.
"So what?" you may say. "It seems all right to me."
All right? For a slave to be praised and applauded
For one noble action, and (rightly) set free,
While his master is punished for just one mistake?
These men are honest, not thugs or defectors—
Just think what a fine contribution they'd make
If you let them: just think how they'd help and protect
    us!

CHORUS:

O comic Muse, come down
And bring our people wisdom;
For the ship of state is foundering,
And only you can save it!

LEADER:

But who am I talking about, someone may ask;
Who are these men I'm so anxious to save?
I'll explain—it's a quite simple task.
We're as eager today to devalue the brave
As our leaders to ill-treat our money.
Once, in our pockets, we'd gold, clean and new,
Fresh-minted, acceptable, yellow as honey—
And we took this fine currency, honest and true,
And devalued it. So, if a man was honest and fair,
We called him old-fashioned, and put all our trust
In second-rate orators, spouting hot air
And looking surprised when their schemes all went
    bust!

176

Ignore them, Athenians! Throw them in jail
And bring back the old stagers. They'll meet the test,
And rule wisely and well. And *then* if we fail,
At least we'll fail honestly, doing our best!

The CHORUS *dance briefly to the accompaniment of a flute.*

SCENE TWO

As the CHORUS *finish,* XANTHIAS *and the* PORTER *come out, chuckling.*

PORTER: No, I don't care what you say, he's a real gent, your master. I can always tell.

XANTHIAS: Huh! Boozing and snoozing, that's all he's good for.

PORTER: No, no . . . I mean, fancy him not thrashing you for pretending you were the master and he was the slave.

XANTHIAS: What? Old fat-belly? I'd like to see him try!

PORTER *wheezing with laughter*: Oh, that's good! That's very good!

XANTHIAS: What d'you mean?

PORTER: That's how a slave ought to talk: calling his master names behind his back.

XANTHIAS: You like that sort of thing too, do you?

PORTER: Nothing better.

XANTHIAS: What about muttering under your breath when he knocks you about?

PORTER: Brilliant!

XANTHIAS: And the keyhole game?

PORTER: What keyhole game?

XANTHIAS: Listening at keyholes when he's talking to his friends . . .

PORTER: And then spreading his private affairs round all the neighbours!

XANTHIAS: That's right.

PORTER: Give us your hand . . . there! I've really taken to you, you know. It's all . . .

He is interrupted by a furious row from inside.

XANTHIAS: My god. What's that?

PORTER *wearily*: Oh, just Aeschylus and Euripides.

XANTHIAS: Oh.

PORTER: I've never known them like it. Time was, the Dead were quiet as the grave . . . now it's fighting and arguing all day long.

XANTHIAS: What about?

PORTER: The thrones.

XANTHIAS: What thrones?

PORTER: The banqueting-thrones, up beside King Pluto.

XANTHIAS: I still don't get it.

PORTER: Look: the best artist, the best singer, the best playwright . . . they each have a throne beside the king, at all the public banquets.

XANTHIAS: Oh.

PORTER: And if someone better turns up, they have to hand them over to him.

XANTHIAS: But what's it got to do with Aeschylus?

PORTER: He's had the Throne of Tragedy for years . . . because he's the best, you see.

XANTHIAS: And you mean . . . someone else . . .

PORTER: You've got it . . . Euripides. As soon as he arrived he started showing off. They're a rough lot down here—bandits, murderers, highwaymen—and they were really impressed when he started rolling the words around. Next thing you know, they go crazy and vote that he's the greatest, and he goes and whips Aeschylus' throne.

XANTHIAS: Why didn't King Pluto throw him out?

PORTER: He couldn't. The crowd were getting nasty . . . demanding a proper trial . . . saying they wanted to see fair play.

XANTHIAS: What? All those robbers and murderers?

PORTER: That's right. Very difficult, it was.

XANTHIAS: And no one supported Aeschylus?

PORTER: There's hardly a man of sense among 'em. They're all from Up There, after all.

XANTHIAS: And what's King Pluto going to do about it?

PORTER: The only thing he *can* do. He's going to have a contest, all legal and official, to decide which of them's the greatest.

XANTHIAS: Just a minute! What about Sophocles? Did no one think of asking him?

PORTER: Ah, Sophocles! There's a real gent for you. When he arrived he shook Aeschylus' hand, and kissed him like a long lost brother. So Aeschylus moves over to make room for him on the throne. But Sophocles won't have it. He's going to be Aeschylus' second: if he wins, that's fine with him, but if Euripides wins he says he'll challenge him and start them all off again.

XANTHIAS: Proper little madhouse, isn't it?

PORTER: You're not joking. Just wait till you see the scales.

XANTHIAS: Scales? What scales?

PORTER: For weighing the lines.

XANTHIAS: Weighing the lines?

PORTER: Yes. Euripides insists it's all done proper, tragedy by tragedy, verse by verse, word by word.

XANTHIAS: Who's the judge going to be?

PORTER: That was the problem: they aren't a very bright lot down here. In any case, Aeschylus doesn't get on too well with the Athenians . . .

XANTHIAS: What—those thieves and bandits? I'm not surprised.

PORTER: And the rest were no better; they wouldn't recognise a poet if they fell over him in the street. So, when your master turned up . . .

XANTHIAS: The god of poetry!

PORTER: That's right. He ought to know something about it, if anyone does.

There is a fanfare from inside the palace.

Oh-oh! They're starting. We'd better get out of the way. Look, I know a nice little pub, just down the road . . .

XANTHIAS: Really? After you . . .

PORTER: No, no, mate . . . *after* you . . .

They go out. There is another fanfare, and a procession comes out of the palace: SLAVES *carrying the scales,* PLUTO *with his royal attendants. During the following choral ode, they all take their places on specially-provided thrones.*

CHORUS:

See how the thunder is gathering, how
The great word-lord is wrinkling his brow
And preparing for battle. His enemy, too,
With his arguments polished and new,
Is eager to tear him in two.

On my right, lofty sentiments, massive and proud;
High prancing epithets, solid and loud;
On my left, a subtler, simpler sound,
A wily wrestler who'll change his ground
And twist his arguments round and round.

180

With his word-mane contemptuously tossed,
And his adjectives rough-hewn, embossed
Like the planks in a shipyard, the lord
Of high rhetoric comes, with a word
Like a tree-trunk, knotted and hard.

His rival, a subtle, slippery customer,
Will take his Muse, and try to fluster her
With clever counter-thrusts; he'll blow
Her art to cobwebs, and show
It's all surface, with nothing below.

As *they finish*, AESCHYLUS *and* EURIPIDES
come out. AESCHYLUS, *a huge man with a bristling
beard and a broad bald head, is too furious to speak.*
EURIPIDES, *a slender ascetic figure, is trying to reason
with him.*

EURIPIDES: I tell you you're wasting your time. It's
mine, and I mean to have it. I'm the better poet—that's
all there is to it.

DIONYSOS: Well, Aeschylus? No comment? You did
hear that, didn't you?

EURIPIDES: Oh, he heard all right. He's always the
same: meaningful pauses, powerful silences. He's just
like one of his own tragedies—the pauses are the best
bits.

DIONYSOS: Hey! That's not very fair.

EURIPIDES: You don't know him like I do. How can I
describe him? Uncouth? Over-elaborate? Torrents of
verbiage? Ask him what *restraint* means, he'd have a
fit . . .

AESCHYLUS *furiously*: Restraint? What do you know
about restraint? What about the beggars *you* favour—
the stench, the filthy clothes, the bed-bugs? Don't talk

181

to *me* about restraint!

DIONYSOS: Hey, hey, calm down! You really will have a fit if you don't take it easy.

AESCHYLUS: Take it easy? Not till I've shown this rag-and-bone man just what I really think of him.

DIONYSOS: Just a minute . . .

AESCHYLUS *ignoring him:* Not only are his choruses more like Cretan belly-dances than anything else, but he *never* . . .

DIONYSOS: Stop! Stop a minute, for goodness sake! Euripides, stand further back, out of range. And you stop all this huffing and puffing, Aeschylus. A fair trial, we agreed on . . . line by line, word by word. Yelling like fishwives won't solve anything.

EURIPIDES: Line by line? Word by word? I'm ready —and so are my tragedies: *Peleus, Aiolos, Meleager, Telephos* . . . all lined up, ready for examination.

DIONYSOS: What about you, Aeschylus? Do you agree?

AESCHYLUS: I suppose so . . . though it's hardly a fair trial.

DIONYSOS: What d'you mean?

AESCHYLUS: When I died, my works lived on . . . I haven't got them by me. But *his* died with him. You heard him say they're all lined up behind him, like an army of scarecrows!

DIONYSOS: Shh! Don't start again! Do you agree to the test, or don't you?

AESCHYLUS: Oh, all right, if you insist.

DIONYSOS: Right. Pick up the libation-jug and the holy water, and call on the gods to help you.

AESCHYLUS *takes the jug, pours a libation, and prays.*

AESCHYLUS:
>   Great Demeter, you gave me what power I have:
>   Let me be a worthy worshipper at your shrine.

DIONYSUS: All right, Euripides: your turn. Here's the incense pot.

EURIPIDES: Er . . . I'd rather not, if you don't mind.

DIONYSOS: Pardon?

EURIPIDES: I've got gods of my own, you see . . .

DIONYSOS: What? Private gods?

EURIPIDES: Yes, and they're a bit fussy . . . they wouldn't care for incense.

DIONYSOS: Well, pray to them their way, then.

EURIPIDES *adopts the posture of the well-known statue of* The Thinker, *and prays:*

EURIPIDES:
>   Air, mother of my soul; tongue-twisting Fire;
>   Intelligence, and clear-headed Intellect,
>   I pray you: help me prove your power today.

DIONYSOS: Is that it?

EURIPIDES: That's it. I'm ready.

DIONYSOS: Good. Aeschylus?

AESCHYLUS: Ready.

DIONYSOS: All right. We'll start with a preliminary statement from each of you. And don't forget, I want a good, clean fight . . . no epigrams below the belt, no playing to the gallery . . . and when I say "break", break.

EURIPIDES: I'll go first, then. I'll talk about my own work in a moment . . . but first I want to show how this word-monger cheats his audiences.

AESCHYLUS: Really! I . . .

DIONYSOS: Shh! Your turn's coming. Go on, Euripides.

183

How does he cheat them?

EURIPIDES: The play begins, and in stalks a great hooded figure, Prometheus or Niobe or someone. And they stand there like stuffed dummies, without saying a word.

DIONYSOS: True enough.

EURIPIDES: All this time the rest of the cast pour out great reams of verse, torrents of words, four odes in a row—and still Niobe says nothing.

DIONYSOS: I must say I thought it was rather effective. The trouble with modern plays is, *everyone* talks *all* the time.

EURIPIDES: No no, you don't understand.

DIONYSOS: Don't I?

EURIPIDES: It's just a cheap trick.

DIONYSOS: Why?

EURIPIDES: Don't you see? Everyone in the theatre on the edge of his seat, waiting for Niobe to say something. The play goes on and on, and what does she say? Nothing.

DIONYSOS: Now now, Aeschylus. Stop jumping up and down like that.

EURIPIDES: Then, about half-way through, when everyone's relaxed again, she whips the cloak off her head, and shouts out a couple of sentences with eyebrows and whiskers on them, like the Big Bad Wolf in a pantomime. No one understands a word she's saying, naturally.

AESCHYLUS: Now *look* . . .

DIONYSOS: Shh! Sit down.

EURIPIDES: It's gibberish from beginning to end.

DIONYSOS to AESCHYLUS: Stop grinding your teeth. (to EURIPIDES) Go on.

EURIPIDES: Gibberish! Scamanders, sepulchres, bronze-clad vulture-eagles . . . words like the walls of a fortress, impossible to batter your way into.

DIONYSOS to AESCHYLUS: He has got a point, you know. I spent several sleepless nights trying to find a tawny horse-cock in my bird-encyclopaedia.

AESCHYLUS: It's a figure-head on ships, you fool!

EURIPIDES: A horse-cock! We write tragedies about horse-cocks now, do we?

AESCHYLUS: All right, what are *your* tragedies about?

EURIPIDES: Not horse-cocks or goat leopards, I can tell you . . . I don't get *my* inspiration off a Persian carpet! No, when you handed Tragedy over to me, she was really in a bad way . . . bloated with adverbs, swollen with participles, so full of syllables she could hardly move. I put her on a diet straight away: pure logic, diluted with a pinch of prosody; carefully-selected metaphors and non-fattening similes. And above all, I came straight to the point. None of this plunging in at the deep end, and wallowing in wordage: the first character that came on the stage told the audience exactly what to expect.

AESCHYLUS *scornfully*: As if they didn't know *that* already!

EURIPIDES: I shall ignore that comment. Secondly: in my plays no one stands about doing nothing. Everyone gets a say: the wife, the slaves, the boss, the daughter-in-law, even old granny in the corner.

AESCHYLUS: Ridiculous!

EURIPIDES: No no, democratic . . . and very educational.

DIONYSOS: Educational?

EURIPIDES: Yes. I mean . . . (*gesturing to the audience*) it taught *them* how to argue.

AESCHYLUS: You can say *that* again!

EURIPIDES: I taught them how to *use* language, and arrange words *neatly* . . . careful thought, cunning examination, logical argument . . . how to look at every-thing twice, leave no stone unturned . . .

AESCHYLUS: You see? No restraint!

EURIPIDES: I kept to ordinary matters in my plays, everyday things we all use, all understand. The audience could follow everything . . . I didn't baffle them with Cycnuses and Memnons, all chariot-knurls and hippo-manic crests! Instead, I taught them to argue logically, to examine their ideas again, and say: "Why's that? Where did I get that from? Who put that in my head?" Can *you* boast as much?

DIONYSOS: Well, can you?

AESCHYLUS *is too angry to answer.* DIONYSOS *goes on gently:*

Come on . . . surely he hasn't outsmarted the Lord of Rhetoric, the greatest word-smith on the tragic stage?

AESCHYLUS *crossly:* Of course he hasn't. I just find it a little annoying to have to bandy words with him at all. I mean, I could crush him with a single adjective . . .

DIONYSOS *hastily:* Now, now . . .

AESCHYLUS: All right. I suppose I'd better say some-thing, or he'll boast that he left me speechless. You . . . fellow . . . just tell me this: what do you consider makes a great poet?

EURIPIDES: Technique, principally, and good sense. We should try and educate our audiences.

AESCHYLUS: All right: let's just think about that for a moment. When I'd finished, my audiences were noble, honest, great-hearted—none of your wine-shop heroes or market-place politicians. People who saw my plays soon thought of nothing but spears and lances, proud fluttering helmet-plumes, greaves, corselets, hearts of solid oak.

DIONYSOS: Steady, Aeschylus. You're losing us again. Can't you explain simply? How did you make them better men?

AESCHYLUS: I wrote a play about war.

DIONYSOS: Which one?

AESCHYLUS: The *Seven Against Thebes*. No one could see *that* without feeling better and braver. Next I wrote the *Persians*, about fighting bravely on till the enemy are destroyed. A good play, that . . . one of my best.

DIONYSOS: Yes . . . I particularly liked that bit about Darius . . . when the chorus clap their hands and shout: "Ee-ow! Ee-ow-oy!"

AESCHYLUS: The greatest poets have always been teachers. Orpheus, Hesiod, Homer . . . they all had something to say. Homer, especially. I like to think my plays owe a lot to Homer. My characters, for example: Patroclus, Achilles, Teucer—great-hearted heroes the audience could learn from. None of your Phaedras and Medeas . . . who can learn anything from a love-sick female?

DIONYSOS: A good point, that.

EURIPIDES: Nonsense! My Phaedras and Medeas never did anyone any harm.

AESCHYLUS: Oh yes they did. Any decent woman seeing them would have rushed off and taken poison.

EURIPIDES: I didn't make their stories up, did I?

AESCHYLUS: No, but you wrote about them. A responsible author would have chosen another subject, not stuck Medea up on the stage so that everyone could sympathise with her. Poets have a duty to set good examples, not bad ones.

EURIPIDES: Good examples? Like your Lykabettuses and Parnassuses? What's the point of a good example no one can understand?

AESCHYLUS: You can't put sublime thoughts in simple language. Great characters need great lines to speak. Not to mention superb costumes . . . though *you* can hardly be expected to understand that.

EURIPIDES: What d'you mean?

AESCHYLUS: Every king that appears in a play of yours is bound to be dressed in rags . . . to make people sorry for him, or something.

EURIPIDES: What's wrong with that?

AESCHYLUS: Nothing, compared to some of the other things you put in. Women marrying their brothers, having babies on the temple steps, and saying things like: "Life just isn't life any more!" Look at the sort of people in Athens nowadays . . . are they like the characters in *my* plays or yours?

EURIPIDES: Now listen . . .

AESCHYLUS: Why, you . . .

DIONYSOS: Break! Stand back! Don't get over-excited . . . there's a long way to go yet.

AESCHYLUS *and* EURIPIDES *retire to opposite corners, and gather their strength during the following ode.*

CHORUS:
How long will this mortal combat last?
The words are flying thick and fast,
As the Olympian strains
Like a horse at its reins,
And his enemy cunningly slips right past!

Don't weaken or yield, however rough
Your opponent: he'll soon cry "Enough!"
If you launch out, and choose

A new line in abuse—
So don't hesitate! Risk some subtle stuff!

Don't be afraid to be clever: tonight
Our audience is extremely bright.
They'll cheerfully follow
Your arguments, swallow
The subtlest of points, and enjoy a good fight.

For days they've been honing their wits
Sharp as razors: they'll all be in fits
If you try something bold,
New-fangled or old,
Intellectual, crammed with clever bits!

DIONYSOS: All right . . . round two. Prologues. Euripides, would you like to begin again?

EURIPIDES: With pleasure. And I shall show, clearly
and concisely, that right from the start our learned friend
is obscure and hard to follow.

DIONYSOS: How, particularly?

EURIPIDES: It's easy. Aeschylus, my dear chap . . .
would you oblige me with the first few lines of the
Oresteia?

There is a murmur of anticipation from the crowd.

DIONYSOS: Shh! Shh! Aeschylus . . . the *Oresteia*.

AESCHYLUS:

"Lord Hermes, who with ever-watchful eye
Hast always guarded this, my father's realm,
Protect me now, and give me thy support;
I have come back, returning home at last."

There is a patter of applause, and he bows.

DIONYSOS: Thank you. Well, Euripides? What's wrong
with that?

EURIPIDES: A dozen things at least.

DIONYSOS: But he's only said four lines.

EURIPIDES: And there are twenty mistakes in each of them.

AESCHYLUS: Now look here . . .

DIONYSOS: Shh! Don't get him angry . . . that's eighty mistakes already.

AESCHYLUS: Really!

DIONYSOS: Shh! It's *his* turn! Now, Euripides . . .

EURIPIDES: I say he's put his foot in it, right from the start.

AESCHYLUS: I'm not having any more of this (*threateningly* to EURIPIDES). Name *one* mistake! Go on, name one mistake!

EURIPIDES: Certainly. Just give me the lines again, would you? I never could remember them.

AESCHYLUS *with loathing*: All right. (*clearing his throat*) Haaarumph!

"Lord Hermes, who with ever-watchful eye
Hast always guarded this, my father's realm,
Protect me now, and give me thy support;
I have come back, returning home at last."

EURIPIDES: Well, there you are. For a start, you keep saying the same thing twice.

AESCHYLUS: What d'you mean, twice?

EURIPIDES: In different words. Listen. "I have come back, returning home at last."

AESCHYLUS: Well?

EURIPIDES: Well, isn't "coming back" the same thing as "returning"?

DIONYSOS: Good heavens, I'd never noticed that!

AESCHYLUS: He doesn't know what he's talking about. It couldn't be better expressed.

EURIPIDES: Please explain.

AESCHYLUS: Orestes has been away, so he "comes back". But he's also been in exile, so he "returns home". The two things are quite different.

DIONYSOS: Brilliant! (aside) I wish I knew what he meant.

EURIPIDES: Give me the next two lines, then.

AESCHYLUS: Oh really!

DIONYSOS: Go on . . . it's his turn.

AESCHYLUS reluctantly:

"On this sad grave I summon thee, grim ghost
Of my dead father. Hear me! Hearken now!"

EURIPIDES: There you go again. "Hear me!" and "Hearken!" . . . the same thing twice.

DIONYSOS: He was talking to a corpse, you fool. Twice, three times . . . he still wouldn't get through.

AESCHYLUS: What about your dialogue, anyway? How do you set about it?

EURIPIDES: I'll show you . . . and if I say anything twice, or you find an unnecessary syllable, I'll eat my manuscripts!

DIONYSOS: That's a very fair offer. Go on, then . . . let's hear one of your prologues.

AESCHYLUS: No no, just a minute! I couldn't bear to go through them all. He writes them to a formula . . . and I can prove it with one little jar of oil.

EURIPIDES: A jar of oil?

AESCHYLUS: A jar of oil. Your lines all have the same rhythm . . . any old words will fit in, a lump of coal, a sack of wool, a jar of oil.

EURIPIDES: Prove it!

AESCHYLUS: All right. Start one of your prologues, and you'll see.

EURIPIDES:

"Aigyptos, as the well-known story tells,
With his fifty daughters in a boat,
Crossing to Argos—"

AESCHYLUS:

Lost a jar of oil.

DIONYSOS: Lost a jar of oil? How unfortunate. Try again, Euripides.

EURIPIDES:

"Great Dionysos, who, in fawn-skins dressed,
And carrying a thyrsos in his hand,
Leads all our revels—"

AESCHYLUS:

Lost a jar of oil.

DIONYSOS: Another jar of oil! It's getting everywhere!

EURIPIDES: Oh no it's not. Let him stick it on this one, if he can:

"True happiness is not for mortal men;
One man, a prince, soon lost his wealth; his friend,
A starving beggar—"

AESCHYLUS:

Lost a jar of oil.

DIONYSOS: Euripides . . .

EURIPIDES *huffily*: Yes?

DIONYSOS: You'd better take in sail a bit . . . there's a storm in an oil-jar blowing up!

EURIPIDES: Rubbish! This one'll finish him . . .

DIONYSOS: All right, but beware of the oil.

EURIPIDES:

"One day Agenor's son, great Cadmus, while
Leaving the city—"

AESCHYLUS:

Lost a jar of oil.

DIONYSOS: It's no use. Give up, before he drowns us in the stuff.

EURIPIDES: Me, give up? Never! I've a hundred more prologues, all oil-proof.

"Once Pelops, son of Tantalus, while on
His way to Pisa—"

AESCHYLUS:
Lost a jar of oil.

EURIPIDES:
"Once great king Oineus—"

AESCHYLUS:
Lost a jar of oil.

EURIPIDES *angrily*: You might at least let me finish the line!

"Once great king Oineus, offering sacrifice
To the gods in heaven—"

AESCHYLUS:
Lost a jar of oil.

DIONYSOS: In the middle of a sacrifice? Awkward.

EURIPIDES *wildly*:
"Zeus, lord of heaven, as the story goes—"

DIONYSOS: No, no! *He'll* lose an oil-jar too! I think the point's been made. I'm tired of prologues, anyway. Time for Round three: Choruses.

EURIPIDES: Choruses? Ah! This is where I really score. He writes terrible choruses, and I can prove it. Just a moment while I get my orchestra . . .

He hurries out.

CHORUS:
What's going to happen now?
How dare he criticise
This man of lofty brow,

This genius, great and wise,
The noblest poet we've ever had?
Beside his plays the rest
Are nothing more than trash—
And *that's* the man this pest
Is fighting! How dim! How rash!
How infinitely *mad*!

EURIPIDES *comes back with a harpist, a flute-player, and a bass drum for himself.*

EURIPIDES: There. Now listen, and I'll give you a sample. This is what all his choruses are like . . .

He beats time for the MUSICIANS, *who play a prelude, and end each couplet with a martial flourish.* EURIPIDES *declaims, beating the drum in time to the rhythm of the words:*

"O Phthian Achilles, men are dying all round you—
Hurry and bring us some help now!
We lake-dwellers honour lord Hermes our master—
Hurry and bring us some help now!
Listen to me, great king of the Greeks, Agamemnon—
Hurry and bring us some help now!"

DIONYSOS *trying to interrupt:* Euripides! Euripi-*des*!
EURIPIDES *ignoring him, carried away:*

"Be silent! The cry is resounding from Artemis' temple—
Hurry and bring us some help now!
Our army is mighty and great, unconquered in battle—
Hurry and bring us some help now!"
One more time! Yes,
"Hurry and bring us some HELP NOW!"
(*Pause*)

There. That's a war-chorus.

194

DIONYSOS: And a thumping noisy one, too.

EURIPIDES: Aha! You want a change, do you? Something quieter? He's pretty good at harp-choruses too.

DIONYSOS: Harp-choruses?

EURIPIDES: Yes. Shall I give you an example?

DIONYSOS: Anything, so long as you keep that drum out of it.

EURIPIDES *signs to the* HARPIST, *who sweeps up and down the strings like a madwoman.*

EURIPIDES:

"When the twin Achaean lords, the kings of Greece,
Oh twang alang-a twang alang!
Sent the dreadful Sphinx to spy on us,
Oh twang alang-a twang alang!
The all-seeing bird, with sword and spear,
Oh twang alang-a twang alang!
Came whirling through the vaults of heaven,
Oh twang alang-a twang alang!
To baffle Ajax,
Twang alang-AH!"

He comes to an abrupt stop. Pause.

There. That was it.

DIONYSOS: That was it? Twang alang-alang? Where did you pick that up, Aeschylus? In a Persian market?

AESCHYLUS: Wherever I picked it up, as you so charmingly put it, at least it's better than the sort of thing *he* writes. What are his choruses, anyway? A ragbag of other men's styles, bits of pub-songs, funeral-dirges, and Carian flute-dances, padded out with lines stolen from Meletos. I'll show you what I mean. Someone give me a lyre. No, no, what am I talking about? These things don't need a lyre . . . a dancing-girl with castanets is more

like it. Here girl, there's a good girl . . . out you come,
don't be afraid . . . puss-puss-puss-puss . . .

A beautiful DANCING-GIRL *comes out, clacking
castanets.*

Ladies and gentlemen, the Muse of Euripides. All right,
my dear, shall we . . . ahem . . . begin?

The GIRL *begins a slow, sinuous dance, clacking her
castanets in time to* AESCHYLUS's *declaiming.*

"Kingfishers, diving, arriving
   At the salt sea spray at the water's edge,
   Chattering, spattering
   Their wings with watery wetness,
   Then flying high where spiders spin,
   Spi-i-i-i-i-i-i-i-in
   Webs woven under the roof-rafters,
   Rafter-roof roof-rafters,
   While the dolphin sings the song
   Sailors smile at,
   Leaping in the wavelets at the sharp ship's bows.
   O grapes! O vine-leaves clustering
   Around the twisted stem—
   O wine, unwearying woe-remover!
   Come, my darling! Come to my loving arms!"
(*spoken, to* DIONYSOS) You noticed that bit, didn't you?
DIONYSOS *gazing at the* DANCING-GIRL: Oh *yes!*
AESCHYLUS *louder*: I said, you noticed that bit there, in
   the last line?
DIONYSOS *jerked back to reality*: I . . . oh . . . yes!
   Yes!
AESCHYLUS: Typical of his lyrics, that. Now I'll give
   you some of his soliloquies.

196

DIONYSOS *hastily*: No no! Spare us the soliloquies, *please*!

AESCHYLUS: You're right. They *are* rather boring. Get the scales ready, then.

DIONYSOS: The scales? What for?

AESCHYLUS: So that I can weigh my works against his. It's the only fair way to settle the argument. Test each phrase, and see how weighty it is.

DIONYSOS: You mean, weigh tragedies like bits of cheese?

AESCHYLUS: That's it exactly.

DIONYSOS: Euripides? What do you think?

EURIPIDES: I told you before: any tests you like, I'm ready.

DIONYSOS *wearily*: All right. Get the scales ready, then.

While the slaves set up the scales, the CHORUS *sing excitedly:*

CHORUS:
   What will these gentlemen think of next?
   You never know what to expect.
   For each one devises
   A hundred surprises
   For his elegant enemy soon to collect.
   It's a good job we're here, and can view
   It ourselves; for if any of you
   Had told us the story
   Of this battle for glory,
   We'd never have thought it was true.

DIONYSOS: The scales are ready. Each of you stand by your weighing-pan.

AESCHYLUS: There.

EURIPIDES: There.

197

DIONYSOS: Now, take a phrase and say it into your pans. And don't let go till I say "Cuckoo!" Ready?

AESCHYLUS: Ready.

EURIPIDES: Ready.

DIONYSOS: Off you go, then . . . one phrase each.

EURIPIDES:

"If only the *Argo* had never sailed . . ."

AESCHYLUS:

"O river Spercheios, where cattle feed . . ."

DIONYSOS: Cuckoo! Let go! Ah! Aeschylus' pan has gone far lower.

EURIPIDES: Why?

DIONYSOS: He put in a whole river . . . like a wool-merchant wetting his stock to make it heavier. You put in a swift, light sailing-ship.

EURIPIDES: Ah! I get the idea now. Let's try again.

DIONYSOS: Take hold, then.

EURIPIDES: Right.

AESCHYLUS: Right.

DIONYSOS: Go!

EURIPIDES:

"Persuasion builds her temple in words alone . . ."

AESCHYLUS:

"Alone of the gods, grim Death accepts no gifts . . ."

DIONYSOS: Cuckoo! His has gone lower again. After all, he threw in Death, the heaviest blow of all.

EURIPIDES: And what about Persuasion? Doesn't that carry any weight?

DIONYSOS: Oh no . . . not compared with Death. Haven't you something really *solid*?

EURIPIDES: H'm . . . I'm not sure . . .

DIONYSOS: It's your last chance.

EURIPIDES: Yes! I've got it!

198

"He took his massive club, bristling with bronze . . ."

AESCHYLUS *quietly*:

"Chariot piled on chariot, corpse on broken corpse . . ."

DIONYSOS: Cuckoo! He's done it again.

EURIPIDES *furiously*: How?

DIONYSOS: Two chariots and two corpses . . . quite a weight.

AESCHYLUS: Look, we're wasting time. So far as I'm concerned he can get into the scales himself, with his wife and kids and all his manuscripts . . . I'll still win, with a couple of well-chosen words.

DIONYSOS *to* PLUTO: My lord, I don't know what to do at all. How can I make a decision? I like them both—Euripides is clever, and Aeschylus is wise . . .

PLUTO: You mean you can't fulfil your mission?

DIONYSOS: Pardon?

PLUTO: You came down here for a poet. One of them must go back with you.

DIONYSOS: I see. All right, you two: I came down for a poet who could help the city. So it's up to you to settle it. Give the city some advice here and now, and I'll take whoever gives the best.

EURIPIDES: In a sentence, you mean?

DIONYSOS: If possible.

EURIPIDES: That's easy. "What you trust, distrust, and start to trust what you distrusted up to now."

DIONYSOS: I'm sorry . . . I don't quite follow . . .

EURIPIDES: Once you trusted certain citizens; now they're in disgrace, and you've got new leaders to look up to. My message is simple: if the new men aren't doing any good, get rid of them and invite the old ones back again.

DIONYSOS: Clever! Yes, I like that. Aeschylus?

199

AESCHYLUS:

"When the enemy's land is yours, and yours
Is his; when you realise ships are wealth
And wealth is ships, this bitter war will end."

Pause.

DIONYSOS: Oh . . . er . . . yes! Quite . . .

PLUTO: Have you chosen, then?

EURIPIDES: Come on, choose—and don't forget you promised to take *me*!

DIONYSOS: "My tongue it was that promised, not my brain," as you so often say. I'll take . . . Aeschylus.

EURIPIDES: What? Why?

DIONYSOS: I think he's the better man. Anything wrong with that?

EURIPIDES: You cheat! You *swore*!

DIONYSOS: Oh yes . . . by "Air, Zeus's mansion" and "The Foot of Time"!

EURIPIDES: You'll leave me here to die?

DIONYSOS *getting a bit confused*: To die, to sleep, perchance to . . . er . . . have dinner?

EURIPIDES: Oh, nuts!

He goes angrily out.

DIONYSOS: Come on, Aeschylus.

PLUTO: Just a minute. Go inside, both of you.

DIONYSOS: Er . . . inside? What for?

PLUTO: Your sandwiches, of course. Never travel without sandwiches, I always say.

DIONYSOS: What a good idea. Come on, Aeschylus.

They go inside.

CHORUS:

There's nothing more useful than a bulging brain.

Look at Aeschylus: has any man so sane
Enjoyed such adulation
From any other nation?
He died, and now he's going to live again.

Not for him the babbling, long and loud,
Of the pea-brained philosophic crowd;
He'll give us dramas
To help us, not harm us,
And build us a city to make us all proud.

PLUTO *comes out again, with* DIONYSOS *and*
AESCHYLUS *in travelling clothes.*

PLUTO: Off you go, then, Aeschylus. They can hardly
wait to see you up there . . . they badly need someone
to give them advice, and educate the backward brethren.
Oh, and talking of backward brethren, tell those politicians—Cleophon, Myrmex, Nikomachos . . . you know,
that crowd—that the sooner they come down to hell the
better everyone'll be pleased. Tell them, if they don't
hurry I'll come up and fetch them myself.

AESCHYLUS: A pleasure. Just make sure that Sophocles
and no one else sits on my throne while I'm away. I won't
have that rag-picker Euripides warming his backside on
my prerogatives!

PLUTO: All right. (*To the* CHORUS) Come on, then:
lift up your torches, and light these gentlemen on their
way with one of your sacred songs.

As DIONYSOS *and* AESCHYLUS *prepare to leave,
the* CHORUS *form a torchlight procession round them.*

CHORUS:
Iacchos! O Iacchos!
Lord of these holy places . . .

They sing quietly behind the LEADER, *who first prays to the gods, then steps forward and addresses the audience.*

LEADER:

Great spirits of hell, allow
Our friends to travel safely home.
And you, ladies and gentlemen, bow
To the wisdom they bring you. Let Peace
Return to the city again,
So that all the crack-brained men
Who never want war to cease
Will have to leave us, and roam
Far beyond the shores of light,
If they want to find someone to fight.

CHORUS:

Iacchos! O Iacchos!
Lord of these holy places, lead the dance
As the Blessed Ones across the stage advance;
Come down and crown our song, we pray—
Dance with us now, and end the play!
Iacchos! O Iacchos!

Everyone goes out in procession, singing.